DrawPlus X3
Resource Guide

The Resource Guide was created and output using Serif PagePlus.

How to contact us

Contacting Serif technical support

Our support mission is to provide fast, friendly technical advice and support from a team of on-call experts. Technical support is provided from our web support page, and useful information can be obtained via our web-based forums (see below). There are no pricing policies after the 30 day money back guarantee period.

UK/International/
US Technical Support: http://www.serif.com/support

Additional Serif contact information

Web:

Serif Website: http://www.serif.com

Forums: http://www.serif.com/forums.asp

Main office (UK, Europe):

The Software Centre, PO Box 2000, Nottingham, NG11 7GW, UK

Main: (0115) 914 2000

Registration (UK only):   (0800) 376 1989

Sales (UK only):   (0800) 376 7070

Customer Service
(UK/International):   http://www.serif.com/support

General Fax: (0115) 914 2020

North American office (US, Canada):

The Software Center, 13 Columbia Drive, Suite 5, Amherst NH 03031, USA

Main: (603) 889-8650

Registration: (800) 794-6876

Sales: (800) 55-SERIF or 557-3743

Customer Service: http://www.serif.com/support

General Fax: (603) 889-1127

International enquiries

Please contact our main office.

Introduction

Welcome to the DrawPlus X3 Resource Guide! Whether you are new to DrawPlus or an experienced user, this guide provides content to help you get the best out of the program.

Offering a range of beginner-level and advanced tutorials, along with full-colour previews of DrawPlus's design templates, samples, and gallery elements, we hope you'll find the Resource Guide a valuable resource that you'll return to time and time again.

The guide is organized into the following chapters:

- **Chapter 1: Tutorials**

  Provides introductory exercises to help new users master the basics, and more advanced tutorials and projects for experienced users.

- **Chapter 2: DrawPlus Gallery**

  This chapter showcases the content provided on the DrawPlus X3 **Gallery** tab. Note that some of this content is provided on the DrawPlus Resource CD.

- **Chapter 3: Design Templates**

  A useful reference gallery showing all of the design templates included on the Resource CD.

- **Chapter 4: Brushes**

  Showcases the natural stroke and spray brushes included in DrawPlus.

- **Chapter 5: Samples**

  A gallery of examples to illustrate the capabilities of DrawPlus.

Contents

Introduction

Tutorials

In this chapter, you'll find a selection of illustrated, step-by-step tutorials and projects, divided into the following categories:

Mastering the Basics—If you're new to DrawPlus, we suggest you start with this section. These exercises allow you to experiment with basic creative tools and techniques. Topics such as shapes, lines, fills, filter effects, and the DrawPlus gallery are explored.

Brushes and Art—Exercises that aim to boost your mastery of the drawing and painting tools and allow you to further experiment with more advanced creative techniques.

Animation and Web—In these tutorials, you'll work with keyframe animation techniques, and learn how to create website content. These exercises vary in complexity from beginner to advanced level.

Projects—The projects reinforce the use of multiple tools and provide a problem/solution approach to creative design challenges.

Accessing the tutorials

You can access the tutorials in one of the following ways:

- From the Startup Wizard, under **View**, click **Browse Tutorials**.
- From DrawPlus, click **Help** and then click **Tutorials**.

Accessing the sample files

To access the sample files that are referred to in the tutorials, you can:

- Click the **Workspace** button on the Tutorials Contents screen.

- or -

- Browse to the **...\Workspace** folder in your DrawPlus installation directory.

  In a default installation, you'll find this folder in the following location:

  C:\Program Files\Serif\DrawPlus\X3\Tutorials\Workspace

Mastering the Basics

In this chapter, you'll find a selection of simple step-by-step exercises, which allow you to experiment with basic creative tools and techniques.

If you're new to DrawPlus, we suggest you start with these tutorials before moving on to the other tutorials.

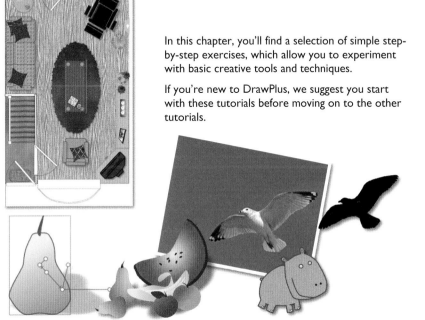

Exploring the Gallery

The DrawPlus **Gallery** tab provides you with a wealth of resources to help you create a multitude of different documents, charts, and drawings.

In this tutorial, we'll introduce you to the **Gallery** and demonstrate how to use its **Layout Symbols** to create a new room layout. We'll also show you how to create a simple greeting card design with Gallery objects.

You'll learn how to:

- Create a scaled drawing to represent your room.
- Place and rearrange room layout elements from the **Gallery** tab.
- Ungroup and edit **Gallery** objects.
- Add bitmap fills, transparency, and filter effects to **Gallery** objects.

💡 You can view our sample files—**Living Room.dpp** and **Greeting Card.dpp**—in the ...**Workspace** folder of your DrawPlus installation. In a typical default installation, you'll find this in the following location:

C:\\Program Files\\Serif\\DrawPlus\\X3\\Tutorials

Let's suppose your living room is 6m long by 4m wide, with a recessed area where two old chairs used to be. You want to rearrange the layout to receive a new 2.25m sofa.

To design a room layout using the Layout Symbols

1   In the Startup Wizard, choose **Drawing**, select a wide A4 or Letter page size and click **Open**.

Now we need to tell DrawPlus what scale to use.

2   Click **Tools**, and then click **Options**.

3   In the **Options** dialog, click the **Drawing Scale** option:

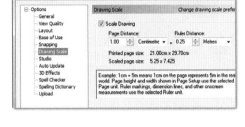

- Select the **Scale Drawing** box.

- Under **Page Distance** enter '1'; select 'centimetres' as the page unit.

- Under **Ruler Distance** enter '0.25'; select 'metres' as the ruler unit.

- Click **OK**.

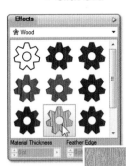

4   On the Quick Shapes flyout, click the **Quick Rectangle** and draw a 6m x 4m rectangle on your page.

5   With the rectangle selected, click the **Effects** tab, then in the category drop-down list, select **Wood**. Click the **Basswood** swatch. You've just created a hardwood floor!

6   To add the recessed area, created by the stairs, place a second smaller rectangle in the lower left corner.

7   To create a 'carpeted' effect:

- On the **Swatch** tab, in the 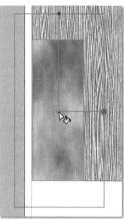 **Gradient** drop-down list, click **Plasma** and apply **Plasma 1**.

- Click the **Fill** tool. On the **Swatch** tab, in the **Palettes** drop-down list, select **Standard RGB**, and then drag a light grey swatch over to replace the white centre node of the fill path.

DrawPlus provides a selection of pre-made room layout elements. For this example we'll place just a few elements, then we'll let you apply the finishing touches yourself.

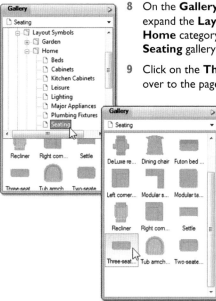

8   On the **Gallery** tab, expand the **Layout Symbols** category, then the **Home** category. Finally, click to display the **Seating** gallery.

9   Click on the **Three-seater sofa** and drag it over to the page. (Notice that when you select and hover your cursor over the object, its page location and dimensions appear on the HintLine toolbar.)

10 Resize the sofa to 2.25 m—to do this you can drag a corner handle or type values into the **Transform** tab.

11 Rotate the sofa and then move it into the recessed area. (To rotate, hover the mouse cursor just outside a corner to temporarily switch to the Rotate cursor, then drag to rotate.)

If any element wasn't installed to your hard drive, you'll be prompted to insert your DrawPlus CD-ROM.

12 Now you can place furniture around the rest of the room.

We added the following elements from the **Gallery** tab:

- From the **Layout Symbols/Home** category—armchairs, TV, coffee table, cabinets, and light fittings.

- From the **Layout Symbols/Garden** category—a selection of plants and pots.

13 The finishing touches— rug, doormat, cushions, candles, photo frame, coffee cups—were all created using QuickShapes with various fills and effects applied.

We'll illustrate a few of these techniques, then leave you to experiment on your own.

You'll notice that we've also changed the 'fabric' of our sofa. On the **Swatch** tab, click the 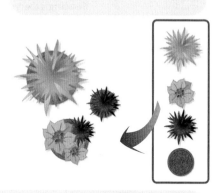 **Bitmap** drop-down list and choose from the wide range of bitmap fills.

The **Garden** category contains a selection of furniture, shrubs, surfaces, etc, that you can use to create garden layouts.

For instructions and design tips, see the *Design a Garden* project.

Cushions

The cushions are **Quick Rectangles**.

1 We converted each shape to curves—on the **Arrange** tab, click ⬤ .

2 Then we used the ⋏ **Node** tool to distort the shapes.

On the **Swatch** tab, in the ▣ ▾ **Bitmap** drop-down list, we chose a selection of fills from the **Material** category.

Stairs and doormat

1 Each stair is a **Quick Rectangle.** To each shape, we applied the **Plasma 1** fill (the same one we used for the large 'carpeted' shape).

2 Then, in the **Filter Effects** dialog, we applied an **Inner Shadow** with the following settings:

- **Opacity** 35
- **Blur** 3.6
- **Distance** 3.6
- **Angle** 104

3 The doormat is another **Quick Rectangle**.

4 We rounded the corners with the  **Node** tool.

On the **Swatch** tab, in the **Bitmap** drop-down list, we chose **Weaves** and applied **weav09**.

Glass coffee table

We dragged the Gallery's **Oblong coffee table** on to our page, then we created a glass effect by applying the following settings:

1 On the **Swatch** tab, change the colour of the line to white.

2 On the **Line** tab, change the weight of the line to 7.5.

3 On the **Effects** tab, in the **Glass** category, apply **Glass 3**.

4 On the **Colour** tab, set the **Opacity** slider to **32%**.

5 In the **Filter Effects** dialog, apply the following:

- **Drop Shadow—Opacity** 35, **Blur** and **Distance** 4.5, **Angle** 135.
- **3D Effects—Blur** 0, **Depth** 375.
- **3D Pattern Map—Blend Mode** Dodge, **Opacity** 100 and **Depth** 24, **Displacement** 80.
- **3D Lighting**—default settings.

The table legs are simple **Quick Ellipses** to which we applied a mid grey fill and line and 60% opacity.

Rug

1 We started with a **Quick Ellipse**.

2 We applied a two colour plasma fill from the **Swatch** tab's **Plasma** category. To create a more subtle effect, we then used the

    Fill tool to adjust the colour of the nodes.

3 We used the **Roughen** tool to create the rug's uneven edge.

4 In the **Filter Effects** dialog, we applied a **Drop Shadow** with the following settings:

   • **Opacity** 35

   • **Blur** 5

   • **Distance** 2.7

   • **Angle** 135

Candles

1 The candles are **Quick Ellipses**.

2 We drew the flames 'by hand' using the  **Pencil** tool.

3 We then applied a plasma fill and used the  **Roughen** tool to create an uneven edge.

Coffee cups

1 We used Quick Shapes for the basic shapes.

2 We applied a light brown fill to the cup.

To create the coffee swirl, we drew a **Quick Spiral**, adjusting the nodes to achieve the desired thickness.

Photo Frame

1 We drew a **Quick Rectangle** and applied a black fill.

2 We imported our photo and 'framed' it in our shape.

3 We selected both objects and clicked Group .

4 On the Drawing toolbar, we selected the **Perspective** tool.

5 On the Context toolbar, we selected the appropriate perspective preset from the flyout.

6 Finally, we used the  **Rotate** tool to rotate our frame. We then positioned it on the cabinet and applied a drop shadow.

Now let's try something completely different. While the DrawPlus design templates include a selection of greeting cards that are ready for you to print out and use, there may be times when you want to create your own personalized card. You can easily do this in DrawPlus—what's more, you don't have to be an artist! In the following section, we'll show you how to create a unique card using elements from the DrawPlus **Gallery** tab.

To create a greeting card using SymbolArt

1   In the Startup Wizard, choose **Drawing**, select **Folded Publications**, then **Tent Card**, and click **Open**.

2   On the **Gallery** tab, in the category drop-down list, expand **Cartoons**, then **Colour**, and finally **Animals**.

3   Drag the **Bird** and **Hippopotamus** images on to your page.

4   Click to select the hippopotamus, then make the image slightly bigger by clicking and dragging a corner sizing handle.

5   With the image still selected, on the **Align** tab, click 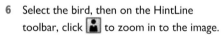 **Centre Vertically** and **Centre Horizontally**.

We're happy with our hippo just the way he is, so let's now move on to the bird.

6   Select the bird, then on the HintLine toolbar, click 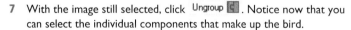 to zoom in to the image.

7   With the image still selected, click Ungroup 🔳 . Notice now that you can select the individual components that make up the bird.

⭐ Some of the gallery objects, such as the Cartoon "Colour" category used in this tutorial, are only found on the Resource CD. If the category is missing, either install it from the CD or alternatively, you can use the animals from the Artistic category. The animals are very similar to the flat, colour version, but the cartoons are created with brush strokes to create detail. Therefore, there will be more individual components to recolour.

8 Click to select the body section. On the **Colour** tab, change the fill and outline colour.

To do this:

- In the upper left corner of the tab, click the **Fill** button, then use the colour wheel to select a new colour to apply to the bird's body (we used **H** 344, **S** 76, **L** 54).

- Click the **Line** button, and then choose a colour for the bird's outline.

9 Repeat as desired to change the colour of any other parts of the bird.

10 When you are happy with the changes you have made, click the **Pointer** tool and draw a selection bounding box around the bird. Below the selection, click Group.

Now that you have regrouped all the elements, you can resize, rotate, and shear them all together.

11 With the bird still selected, drag a corner handle and resize the image so that it is small enough to sit on the hippo's head.

12 On the Hintline toolbar, click **Zoom Out** until you can see the entire image.

13 Select the hippo and the bird and click Group.

14 On the Drawing toolbar, click the **Shadow** tool.

15 In the Context toolbar, apply the following settings:

- **Opacity** 20
- **Blur** 35
- **Shear X** 0.0 ; **Shear Y** 0.0
- **Scale X** 130 ; **Scale Y** 20

16 Finally, on the Text flyout, click the **A** **Artistic Text** tool and type a caption for your image.

💡 You can also drag the nodes with the pointer tool to change the shadow. See online Help for more details.

Use the **Text** context toolbar and **Swatch** tab to change the font style, size, and colour as required. This is covered in detail in the "*Mastering the Basics: Working with Text*" tutorial.

That's all there is to it! You've created a simple, but effective unique greeting card design.

best friends forever...

Now that you've seen how easy it is to place and adjust **Layout Symbol** images, and edit Gallery objects, you can apply the same technique to any item in the DrawPlus Gallery. Have fun!

💡 We limited our editing to changing line and fill colour. However, you can change just about anything. For example, if you wanted to, you could give the bird extra long legs and make him nip the ear of the hippo...

To create the divided beak

1 Resize the beak shape to make it narrower.

2 Copy and paste this new smaller beak and on the Arrange tab, click ▷ **Flip Vertical**.

3 Rotate and position the beak sections.

4 Select the lower beak shape and click 🔳 **Send to Back** to move it behind the hippo's ear.

Working With Text

DrawPlus offers three types of text to use in your projects.

In this tutorial, we'll show you how to:

- Work with artistic, frame and shape text.
- Create, edit, and format all types of text.
- Create text-on-a-path.
- Change the shape and fill of text frames.

Working With Text

DrawPlus offers *frame text, shape text* and *artistic text*. You can use the same methods to perform operations such as selecting, editing, and formatting both types of text. However, there are a few differences, as outlined in the following table.

Frame text:
- Lets you flow text between multiple text frames.
- Can be shaped into familiar QuickShape objects.
- Is generally used for longer passages of text, or non-decorative text such as contact details, product information, etc.
- The frame can be resized without altering the text properties.

Shape text:
- Adds text to any placed object, without creating a separate text object.
- The container can be resized without affecting the text properties.
- Is generally used for short, non-decorative text such as labels.

Artistic text:
- Lets you stretch or squash the text by dragging its container.
- Allows you to create shaped text effects by putting the text on a path.
- Allows you to edit the text positioning at a character level.
- Is especially useful for titles, pull quotes, and other special-purpose text.

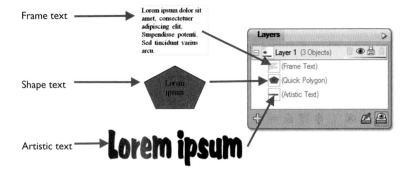

Frame text

Shape text

Artistic text

In this tutorial, we'll show you how to create and manipulate the three types of text. We'll be working with the greeting card project that we created in the "*Mastering the Basics: Exploring the Gallery*" tutorial. If you haven't yet completed this project, you can use the **greeting card.dpp** file included in the **Workspace** folder.

To open an existing project file:

1   On the **File** menu, click **Open**.

2   In the **Open** dialog, browse to the **Workspace** folder.

In a typical default installation, you'll find this in the following location:

C:\Program Files\Serif\DrawPlus\X3\Tutorials

3   Click on the **greeting card.dpp** file and then click **Open**.

To begin, we'll show you how to select, edit, and format text.

The methods described in the following sections are applicable to artistic, shape and frame text.

To select and edit text:

1   Using the **⬆ Pointer** tool, click to select the text object located beneath the cartoon.

In the lower-left corner of the workspace, the HintLine toolbar tells us that this is *artistic text*.

2   On the Drawing toolbar, select the **A Artistic text** tool.

3   Click and drag to select the first letter of the word 'Best.'

The selected text is highlighted in blue.

4   Type a lowercase 'b.'

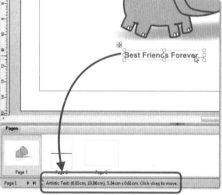

5 Repeat step 3 to change the other uppercase letters to lowercase.

To format text:

1 Triple-click anywhere on the line of text you've just edited to select the entire line.

2 At the top of the workspace, on the Text context toolbar:

- Click to expand the Font drop-down list and set the font to something bold and fun looking. We chose Apple Boy BT.

- Click to expand the **Point Size** drop-down list and set the point size to 72 pt. (You can also type a value directly into the box and press the **Enter** key.)

- Remove the bold formatting from the text by clicking **B** **Bold**.

3 With the text object still selected, drag the centre-right resize handle inwards.

Notice how the text appears to squash in relation to its container.

Drag the handle outwards to expand the text until you are happy with the effect.

To apply a gradient fill:

1   With the text still selected, go to the **Swatch** tab.

2   Expand the **■ ▼** **Gradient Fills** flyout and select **Linear**.

Click the **Linear 22** swatch to apply it to the text.

This gradient fill works well with our card, so we don't need to change it. However, if required, you can edit both the fill path and the colours used in a gradient fill.

The following procedure is optional.

To edit a gradient fill:

1   Select the text object and then on the Drawing toolbar, click the **◈** **Fill** tool.

The object's fill path is displayed.

2   You can adjust the fill path:

   • To change the colour spread, click and drag the fill path nodes.

- To change the colour of a fill path node, select it and then on the **Swatch** tab, click a colour swatch.

- or -

Drag from a colour swatch on to any node to change the key colour of the node. Note that the node doesn't need to be selected.

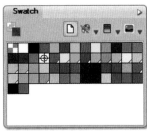

In our example, we used the **Document** palette to apply the colour used for the bird's body **(H 337, S 75, L 53)** to the leftmost node, and bird's outline colour **(H 244, S 100, L 50)** swatch to the rightmost node.

Now let's create a new artistic text object...

To create artistic text:

1   In the **Pages** tab, click to select page 3.

2   On the Drawing toolbar, click the **A** **Artistic Text** tool.

3   Click and drag on the page to set the font size to approximately 16pt.

4   On the Text context toolbar, in the **Font** drop-down list, select Apple Boy BTN.

5   On the **Swatch** tab, select the **Fill** button and click a black swatch.

6 Type 'the cute and cuddly card company'.

7 With the new text object selected, drag it into the lower-left third section of the card.

To do this, drag the 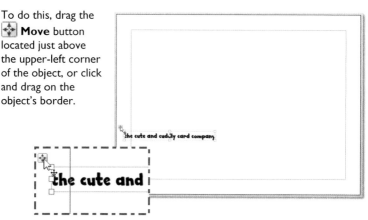 **Move** button located just above the upper-left corner of the object, or click and drag on the object's border.

Next, we'll fit our text to a curved path.

To put text on a path:

1 With the text object still selected, on the Text context toolbar, expand the **Path Text** flyout and click to apply the **Curved Text - Top Circle** preset.

2 To adjust the path, on the Drawing toolbar, click the **Node** tool.

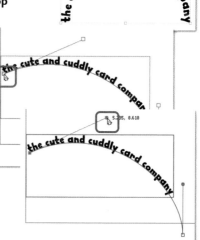

3 Stretch out the text path slightly by dragging the Start and End nodes.

4 (Optional) To adjust the slope of the path, click on a Start or End node and then drag the curve handle.

When you've finished adjusting your text path, it should resemble the illustration. (We also added a cute rabbit from the **Gallery** tab.)

Now let's make the inside of our card a little more interesting. In the following sections, we'll create some frame and shape text. (These procedures work equally with artistic text).

To create shape text:

1   In the **Pages** tab, click to select page 2.

2   On the Drawing toolbar, from the 🔲▾ **QuickShapes** flyout, click to select the **Quick Heart** shape.

3   Click and drag on the centre of the lower page to draw a heart and from the **Colour** or **Swatch** tab, choose a pink colour fill.

4   With the shape still selected, on the Drawing toolbar, click the **A Artistic Text** tool.

An insertion point will begin to flash within the shape. Type "best friends forever..."

5   With the  **Pointer** tool, click and drag on the shape's resize handles to change the size of the shape. Notice how the text size stays the same but the wrap changes.

6   Adjust the heart so that it is approximately 5cm by 5cm and place it in the centre of the bottom half of the page.

The shape is almost complete, but we could change the font a little to make it more effective.

To change font:

1   With the shape selected, click the **A** **Artistic Text** tool.

2   Triple-click on the shape text to select it.

3   On the Text context toolbar, in the **Fonts** drop-down list, select a bold, fun font.

    We chose **Apple Boy BT** and increased the font size to 16 pt.

    We also applied a white fill from the **Swatch** tab.

Let's finish by creating a new text frame.

To create a text frame:

1   In the **Pages** tab, click to select page 3.

2   On the Drawing toolbar, on the Text Frames flyout, click the **Frame Text**.

3   In the lower-right corner of the card, click and drag to create a small text frame.

4   On the Text context toolbar, select **Arial** font, **12 pt**.

5   On the **Swatch** tab, click the black swatch.

6 Type 'Created with DrawPlus X3 ' then resize and position the text frame as required. Notice that if you resize the text frame the text stays the same size and shape. This is because it is Frame text.

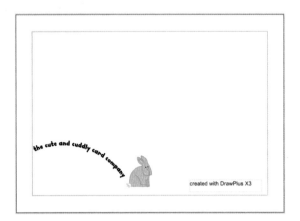

(Optional) To adjust the shape and fill of a text frame:

1 In the **Pages** tab, click to select page 2.

2 On the Drawing toolbar, on the Text Frames flyout, click the 📄 **Frame Text**.

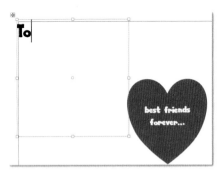

3 Click and drag to create a text frame approximately 7cm by 7cm.

4 On the Text context toolbar, select **Apple Boy BTN** font, **30 pt**.

5 On the **Swatch** tab, click the black swatch.

6 Write "To" in the frame.

Now we're going to change the shape of the text frame to match the heart in the middle of the card.

7   On the Drawing toolbar, click the  **Pointer** tool and click to select the text frame.

8   On the **Swatch** tab, apply a pink fill. (We used **RGB 255, 218, 255**.)

9   On the Drawing toolbar, click the **Node** tool and on the Context toolbar, choose **Quick Heart** from the Shaped frame drop-down menu.

10 Repeat steps 2-9 to create a "From" text frame.

Although the heart text frame looks very similar to the shaped text frame we created earlier, the heart text frame appears as a text object in the Layers tab. Unlike shaped text, text frames can be linked together to flow between different frames.

See online Help for information about adjusting text flow and linking frames.

For more creative uses of text, why not try the tutorials *Creating a Cartoon Movie Poster* and *Creating an Animated Banner*.

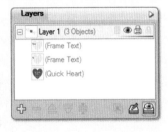

That's it, your card is complete!

You now know how to edit and format text, apply text effects, create text-on-a-path, and create new artistic, shape and frame text objects.

The skills you have acquired should be sufficient for most of your DrawPlus projects, but you'll find more detailed information in online Help.

Working with Line Tools

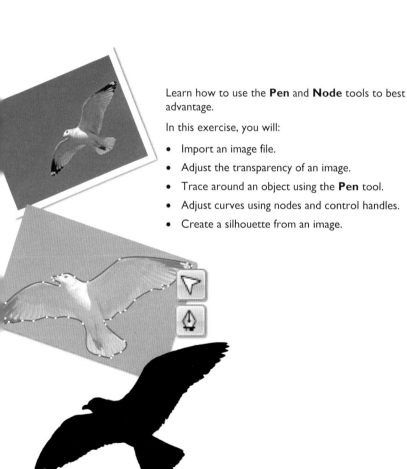

Learn how to use the **Pen** and **Node** tools to best advantage.

In this exercise, you will:

- Import an image file.
- Adjust the transparency of an image.
- Trace around an object using the **Pen** tool.
- Adjust curves using nodes and control handles.
- Create a silhouette from an image.

In this tutorial, we'll be tracing around an object with varied curves, using an imported photo of a bird.

1 In the DrawPlus Startup Wizard, choose **Drawing**. Select a page size of your choice and click **Open**.

2 On the Drawing toolbar, click  **Insert Picture**. In the **Insert Picture** dialog, browse to locate the **bird.jpg** file in your **Workspace** folder.

   In a typical default installation, you'll find this in the following location:

   C:\Program Files\Serif\DrawPlus\X3\Tutorials

   Click on the **bird.jpg** file, and then click **Open**.

3 Click on your page to place the photo at actual size.

   On the HintLine toolbar, click ■ **Zoom In** or drag the Zoom slider to zoom into the image.

4 On the Drawing toolbar, click the ◔ **Pen** tool.

   At the left of the Pen context toolbar, notice that the **Pen** tool has two creation modes:

   - ⌒ **Smooth joins**

   - ⌃ **Sharp joins**

   These options let you create smooth curve or sharp 'cusp' points as you lay down the nodes that make up your curve. As our image is predominantly comprised of curves, we'll work in **Smooth joins** creation mode.

5 On the context toolbar, click ⌒ **Smooth joins**.

💡 You can make the image easier to trace around by reducing opacity. To do this, select the image and then on the **Colour** tab, set the **Opacity slider** to 50%.

6 Click where the wing meets the head, then continue clicking to place 'nodes' around the outline.

(You don't have to be exact; we'll tidy up later.)

The images right and below show the order of the places we clicked to trace the outline of the bird in an anti-clockwise direction. Note that we used a 3pt red line for clarity.

You can make the shape as complicated or as simple as you wish.

This tutorial steers a middle course—but it can be done with fewer or more nodes.

7 When you reach the last node (18 in our example), close the shape.

On the Line context toolbar, click ⊬ **Close Curve**.

-or-

Hover over the last node and click when the cursor changes to 🖊 °.

When you have completed your outline, you will probably find that some areas of your curve need to be adjusted.

We'll do this next by adjusting nodes, curve segments, and control handles.

8 On the Drawing toolbar, click the 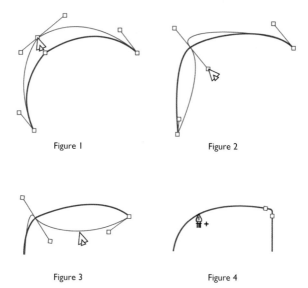 **Node** tool, or with the **Pen** tool still selected, hold down the **Ctrl** key to switch temporarily to the **Node** tool.

There are various ways to reshape your outline using this tool:

- To shape a curve using a node, simply click and drag it (Figure 1).

- To shape a curve using a control (Bézier) handle, click and drag the handle ends (Figure 2).

- To shape a curve segment (the portion of a curve between two nodes), click on the curve segment and drag it (Figure 3).

- To add a node, click at the point where you want to add the node (Figure 4).

Experiment with these techniques to fine-tune your outline.

Figure 1   Figure 2

Figure 3   Figure 4

Before we end this tutorial, let's look at another way to use nodes to shape a curve.

Node types

As we've just seen, curves consist of curve segments, nodes and control handles. When you click on a node, the ◢ ◪ ⋀ ⋂ ⋀ **node type** buttons become available for selection from the context toolbar. The behaviour of the control handles, and the curvature of the segments on either side of a node, depend on whether the node is sharp, smooth, symmetric, or smart.

- ◪ **Sharp Corner:** Curve segments either side of the node are completely independent.

- ◪ **Smooth Corner:** The slope of the curve is the same on both sides of the node (the depth of the two joined segments can be different).

- ⋂ **Symmetric Corner:** Nodes join curve segments with the same slope and depth on both sides of the node.

- ⋀ **Smart Corner:** Nodes automatically determine slope and depth for a rounded, best-fitting curve.

(See 'Changing nodes and line segments' in the 'Editing lines and shapes' online Help topic.)

When you click to place a node, as we did in this exercise, the default node type is **Smart Corner** (when you edit its control handles, both sides of the curve at that point will react in the same way).

When you click and drag to place a node, the default node type is **Smooth Corner**.

⚠ If you adjust the control handles of a **Smart Corner** node, it switches to a **Smooth Corner**. You can reset the node type on the context toolbar—but if you want to maintain your smart corners, be careful what you click and drag!

If you have copied the nodes that we created to make our outline, you will probably have an area of wing that is too straight. If you drag the line out to curve it, the other part of the line will also change. First, we need to change the node type. Let's do this now.

💡 To see how these node types behave, create a new curve, hold down the **Ctrl** key and select a node, and then switch between the various node types. In some cases, the curve will change as soon as the new node type is clicked, in other cases, you'll need to drag the control handles to see how the behaviour changes.

To change node type

1   Click the 🔽 **Node** tool, select the object and then select the node you want to change (**Shift**-click to select multiple nodes).

2   On the context toolbar, click 🖊 **Sharp corner** to change the node type.

3   To shape the line to the wing, click and then drag the Bézier handle until the line follows the edge. Alternatively, click on the curve segment and drag it into place.

4   Repeat steps 2-3 to adjust any other lines.

To complete our design, we changed the line colour to black, and applied a black fill on the **Swatch** tab to create a silhouette.

What you do with your outlined shapes is entirely up to you. Try modifying the colours, adding colour fills, or applying 3D effects to customize the objects.

Mastering the Pen and Node tools open up endless possibilities for your artwork. They are definitely worth persevering with. Good luck!

Working with
Shapes and Fills

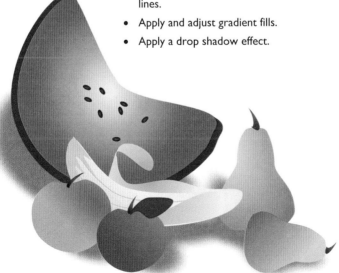

This quick and easy tutorial will show you how to turn a simple shape into a piece of fruit!

In this exercise, you will:

- Create QuickShapes.
- Use the **Pen** tool.
- Use the **Node** tool to transform shapes and lines.
- Apply and adjust gradient fills.
- Apply a drop shadow effect.

- In the Startup Wizard, choose
  Drawing, select a page size of your
  choice and click **Open**. We'll draw a
  few different fruit shapes, let's begin
  with a pear.

💡 To constrain the shape, press and hold the **Shift** key while you draw. (You don't need perfect shapes for this exercise however.)

To draw a pear

1 On the Drawing toolbar, on the Quick
  Shapes flyout, click the 🔘 **Quick
  Ellipse** and draw an ellipse on your
  page.

2 On the Drawing toolbar, click the
  🔽 **Node** tool.

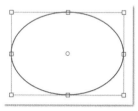

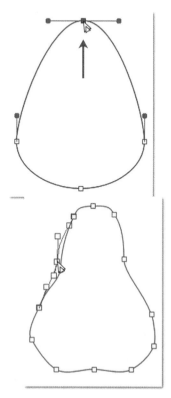

3 With the shape selected, click **Tools
  > Convert to Curves**. You'll see
  four 'nodes' appear on the circle's
  edge.

  Converting a shape to curves allows
  you to edit it using the **Node** tool
  and the **Curves context toolbar**.

  - To change the shape of an object
    that has been converted to curves,
    click one of its nodes and then
    drag it to a new position.

  - To add a node, click a line segment
    with the **Node** tool to add a new
    node at that point.

  - To delete a node, select it with the
    Node tool and press the **Delete**
    key or click the ⬛ **Delete Node**
    button on the Context toolbar.

4 Use the **Node** tool to add and move
  nodes, until your shape resembles a
  pear.

If you're having trouble with this step, you can use our sample file, **Pear.dpp**, which you'll find in the **Workspace** folder of your DrawPlus installation directory—normally located at:

C:\Program Files\Serif\DrawPlus\X3\Tutorials

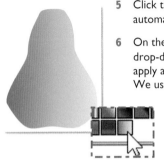

5   Click the **Pointer** tool. Your shape is automatically selected.

6   On the **Swatch** tab, in the **Gradient** drop-down list, select the **Linear** category and apply any yellow/green fill by clicking its swatch. We used **Linear 185**.

If you want to change the colour or gradient of the fill path, you can do so by using the **Fill** tool. We'll show you how to do this next, but if you're happy with the colour of your pear you can skip the following step.

7   On the Drawing toolbar, click the **Fill** tool.

Depending on the type of fill you selected (linear, radial, ellipse, etc.), you'll see the fill path displayed as one or more lines, with nodes marking where the spectrum between each key colour begins and ends.

You can edit the fill path by:

• Dragging the nodes to change the spread of colours between nodes.

• Changing, adding, or deleting key colours.

To change the colour spread

Drag the start and end path nodes, or click on the object for a new start node and drag out a new fill path. The gradient starts where you place the start node, and ends where you place the end node.

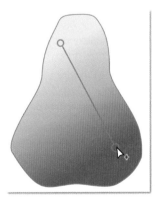

💡 When dragging from colour swatches to nodes, make sure the tip of the pointer is over the node or path (watch the cursor) when you release the mouse button. Otherwise the colour will be applied to the whole object as a solid fill.

To change a key colour

Click its node, then click a colour swatch.

- or -

Drag from a colour swatch on to any node to change the key colour of the node. Note that the node doesn't need to be selected.

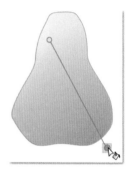

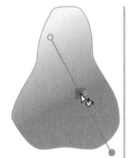

To add a key colour

Drag from a colour swatch on to a portion of the fill path where there is no node. The cursor changes to include a plus (+) sign.

To delete a key colour

Select a colour node and press **Delete**.

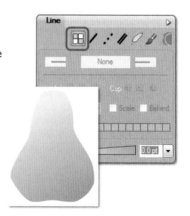

8   On the **Line** tab, remove the outline from the pear by clicking ⊞ **No line**.

To complete the pear, all we need to do now is draw the stalk.

9   On the Drawing toolbar, click the 🖊 **Pen** tool and then draw the outline of the stalk on your page.

Be sure to connect the first and last nodes to create an enclosed shape.

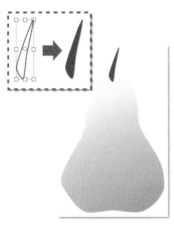

10 Click the 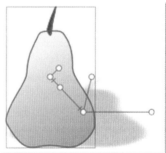 **Pointer** tool, then on the **Colour** or **Swatch** tab, apply a dark green line and fill to the shape.

11 Finally, drag the stalk into position on top of the pear.

For a touch of realism, we'll use the **Shadow** tool to add a drop shadow effect.

To add a drop shadow

1 On the **Edit** menu, choose **Select All** (or press **Ctrl + A**), then to the lower right of the selection, click Group 🔲 .

2 With the pear selected, on the Drawing toolbar, click the 🔳 **Shadow** tool.

On the Shadow context toolbar, set the following values, pressing the **Enter** key after each one:

- **Opacity:** 25
- **Blur:** 17
- **Shear X:** 7
- **Scale X:** 155%
- **Scale Y:** 50%

(You can also drag the various Shadow tool nodes to adjust the effect.)

You've created your first fruit shape. We think you'll agree that this was a very simple process. Let's now try our hand at drawing a watermelon slice.

To draw a watermelon slice

1   On the QuickShapes flyout, click the
    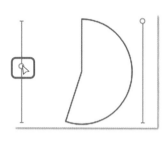 **Quick Ellipse** and draw an
    ellipse on your page.

2   With the shape selected, drag the left
    node down to almost the halfway
    point.

3   On the **Tools** menu, click **Convert
    to Curves**.

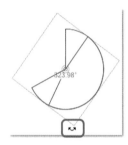

4   Hover the cursor just outside one of the
    corners of the shape. When the cursor
    changes to the Rotate cursor, rotate the
    shape by clicking and dragging one of the
    rotate handles.

5   Click the ⬉ **Pointer** tool, then right-click
    your shape and click **Copy**. Right-click again
    and click **Paste**.

A copy of the shape is pasted on top
of the original and is selected by
default.

6   Make this new shape slightly smaller
    than the original by dragging one of
    its corner size handles towards the
    centre.

7   Place the shapes so that they match
    up along the cut edge of the slice.

8   Select the large shape, then on the
    Swatch tab, apply a dark green fill
    and outline.

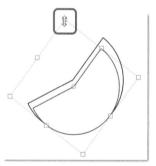

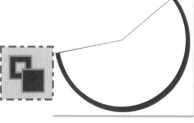

9 Select the small shape, then on the **Swatch** tab, in the 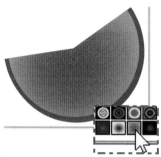 **Gradient** drop-down list, select **Radial** and apply an orange/red fill—we used **Radial 154**.

10 On the **Line** tab, remove the outline by selecting **None** from the line style drop-down list.

Now all that remains is to add some seeds...

11 Create a narrow ellipse and fill it with an appropriate radial fill.

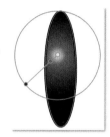

We used **Radial 155** and added a white node to the fill path. We also adjusted the angle of the fill path slightly.

12 Copy and paste this shape to make additional seeds. Rotate the seeds and vary their positions inside the watermelon slice.

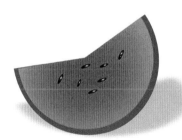

13 Add a drop shadow and you're done!

You can use this basic method to draw any other kind of fruit or vegetable.

The banana is slightly more complicated, however, so we'll break it down for you...

If you want to dissect this image for yourself, you'll find the sample file, **Banana.dpp**, in the **Workspace** folder.

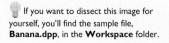

To draw a banana

This section explains how we drew our banana; however, don't feel you have to use the same method. Experiment with the various tools and techniques that DrawPlus has to offer—you may find a better way to create the same effect.

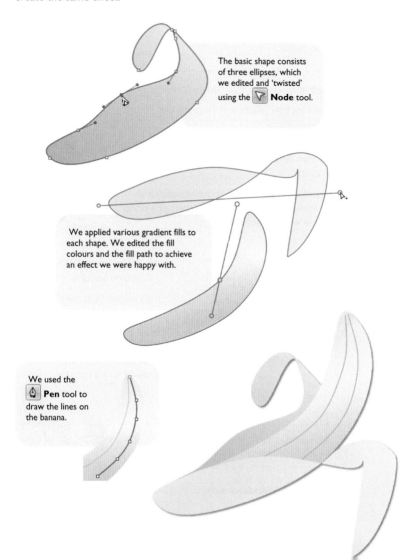

The basic shape consists of three ellipses, which we edited and 'twisted' using the Node tool.

We applied various gradient fills to each shape. We edited the fill colours and the fill path to achieve an effect we were happy with.

We used the Pen tool to draw the lines on the banana.

The shading effects on the banana and skin were created with the 🖉 **Pencil** tool. We created closed shapes by connecting the start and end nodes, and then applied various solid and gradient fills.

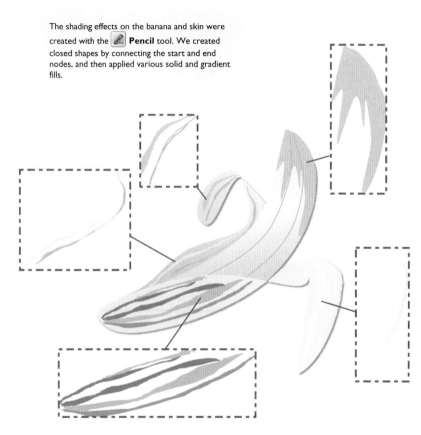

As you can see, with DrawPlus you don't need to be an expert to produce effective results. All it takes is a few simple shapes, lines, and fills, and a little practice. Once you've drawn your individual fruit shapes, you can group them any way you like to create interesting still-life compositions.

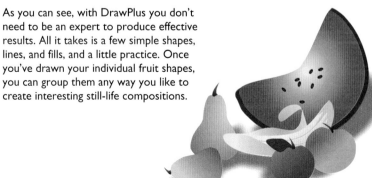

Brushes & Art

This section includes exercises that aim to boost your mastery of the natural media and spray brushes, and allow you to experiment with the creative techniques provided in the Cutout Studio and AutoTrace environments.

Using the Natural Media Brushes

DrawPlus provides you with an exciting range of possibilities for creating natural looking artistic effects. The **Brushes** tab contains a vast array of pressure-sensitive brush strokes—a powerful set of tools that dramatically expands your potential for creativity by allowing you to create effects such as pencil sketches, charcoal drawings, and watercolours.

In this tutorial, we'll introduce you to this exciting collection of drawing tools and show you how you can use them to create natural-looking effects with ease.

You'll learn how to:

- Use the **Brushes** tab, **Paintbrush** tool and **Brush** context toolbar.

- Apply and edit brush strokes using the mouse.

- Change brush stroke attributes such as width, colour, smoothness, and opacity.

- Set brush stroke defaults.

The ✏ natural stroke brushes on the DrawPlus **Brushes** tab are intended to mimic the strokes created by 'real' paintbrushes, pens, pencils, and charcoal crayons. This means that when you select a particular brush, you should use it in the same way you would use the traditional art medium it represents. (For details on using the spray brushes, see the *Brushes & Art: Using Spray Brushes* tutorial.)

The aim of this tutorial is to show you how to use the brushes in your drawings. We'll demonstrate a couple of techniques and illustrate how you can create different effects by adjusting brush stroke style and attributes.

💡 You can create your own custom brushes and add them to the **Brushes** tab.

See the *Brushes & Art: Making New Brushes* tutorial, available from the Tutorials contents screen (to open the contents screen, click **Help > Tutorials**).

Let's start by exploring the various tabs, tools, and controls that you'll be using:

- The **Brushes** tab
- The 🖌 **Paintbrush** tool
- The **Brush context toolbar**

The Brushes tab

Use the **Brushes** tab to select the natural media effect you want to use. DrawPlus provides many different brush styles from which to choose. Brush styles are divided into categories. Simply select a category from the drop-down list and then click a brush style swatch. Once you have chosen your brush style you can:

- Adjust the width of your stroke—on the **Line** tab, type a value or drag the slider. (Note that if the **Paintbrush** tool is the active tool, you can also set the brush width on the **Brush context toolbar**. See the following sections.)

- Change the colour of your brush stroke—at the top left of the **Swatch** or **Colour** tab, click to activate the **Line** option and then click a colour to apply it.

The Paintbrush tool

Select the 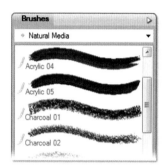 **Paintbrush** tool to apply a brush stroke from the **Brushes** tab.

To use the Paintbrush tool

1 On the Drawing toolbar, click the **Paintbrush** tool.

2 On the **Brushes** tab, in the brush category drop-down list, select the **Global > Natural Media** category.

3 In the brush style list, click the swatch for the brush stroke you want to use.

4 Use your mouse or pen and tablet to apply the brush stroke to your page.

To draw and edit brush strokes using a mouse

- To create a brush stroke, click where you want the brush stroke to start and then hold the mouse button down as you paint. The stroke appears immediately and follows your mouse movements.

- To end the brush stroke, release the mouse button.

- To extend the brush stroke, select the stroke with the **Paintbrush,** then position the mouse cursor over one of the stroke end nodes. The cursor changes to include a plus symbol. Click on the node and drag to add a new segment.

- To redraw any part of the stroke, select it with the **Node** tool, and then click and drag the node to the new position.

When painting with the **Paintbrush,** you can temporarily switch to the **Node** tool by holding down the **Ctrl** key. This allows you to edit the nodes and control handles of your strokes as you go. To continue painting, simply release the **Ctrl** key.

To draw and edit brush strokes using a pen and tablet

- To create a brush stroke, use the pen and tablet exactly as you would use a 'real' pen or paintbrush on paper or canvas. Press down on the tablet where you want the stroke to start, and hold it down as you paint. The stroke appears immediately and follows your pen movements.

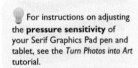 For instructions on adjusting the **pressure sensitivity** of your Serif Graphics Pad pen and tablet, see the *Turn Photos into Art* tutorial.

If you need help with installation, or other customization issues, see the *Serif Graphics Pad User Manual*.

- To end the brush stroke, simply lift the pen off the tablet.

- To extend the brush stroke, position the pen cursor over one of the end nodes. The cursor changes to include a plus symbol 🖉. Press down on the node and drag the pen to add a brush stroke segment.

- To redraw any part of the brush stroke, press and hold the **Ctrl** key and then click on a node and drag the stroke segment to the new position.

- Use the accompanying **Brush context toolbar** and **Pressure** tab to customize your brush strokes as you create them, as well as to edit brush strokes that you have already created. We'll discuss this in the following sections.

To move a **group of nodes** on a brush stroke segment:

- Click the **Node** tool and draw a selection box around the nodes you want to move.

- Click and drag one of the selected nodes to move the whole group.

The Brush context toolbar

When you create a brush stroke with the **Paintbrush** tool, the **Brush context toolbar** displays a selection of controls that you can use to adjust the appearance of the stroke.

| Brush: | ♦ Line Colour | Width: ⬍ 0 pt | ▸ | Opacity: ⬍ 100% | ▸ | Smoothness: ⬍ 60% | ▸ | ● |

Brush

This box displays the swatch for the brush style you select on the **Brushes** tab. Clicking the box opens the **Brush Edit** dialog, which you can use to make changes to a brush stroke. For example, you can adjust the size of the **Head**, **Body**, and **Tail** sections, or change the method used to repeat the body section.

(Editing brush strokes is beyond the scope of this tutorial. For more information, see online Help or the *Brushes & Art: Making New Brushes* tutorial, available from the Tutorials contents screen.)

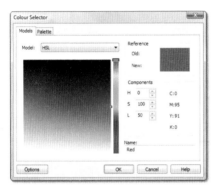

Colour

Clicking this button opens the **Colour Selector** dialog. Here you can edit the line colour of your brush stroke.

For more information on defining and editing colours, see the online Help.

Width

This box displays the width, or thickness, of a brush stroke. To adjust the thickness, click the ⬍ arrows, or click the arrow to the right of the value box and then drag the slider.

Opacity

This box displays the opacity of a brush stroke. To adjust opacity, click the Up and Down arrows or click and drag the slider.

Our example shows the same stroke with 100%, 50%, and 25% opacity.

Smoothness

This box displays the smoothness of a brush stroke. To make a brush stroke more or less smooth, click the ⬆⬇ arrows or click and drag the slider.

0% smoothness

80% smoothness

Select-on-Create

- If this button is **selected**, when you release the mouse button or take your pen off the tablet, the brush stroke you just created is automatically selected, allowing you to easily add to or edit it.

- If this button is **not selected**, when you release the mouse button or take your pen off the tablet, the brush stroke you just created is not selected. If you want to edit or add to the brush stroke, you must first click on it with the **Paintbrush or Node** tool.

Fill-on-Create

Select this button if you want to fill shapes and curves as you create them with your brush.

💡 When you have created a brush stroke, you can select and edit it as just you would any other object on your page.

Similarly, when you select a brush stroke, the controls that display on the context toolbar will change depending on the particular tool you are using.

For example, try selecting a brush stroke with the **Paintbrush** tool, the ▶ **Pointer** tool, and the ⑄ **Node** tool—as you switch from one tool to the next, you'll see a different set of controls displayed in the context toolbar.

Setting the default brush stroke

When you create any new object in DrawPlus, its appearance depends on the current **default settings** for the particular type of object.

Properties for brush strokes include width, colour, opacity, and smoothness. The term **default brush stroke** refers to the properties of the brush stroke that will be applied to the next new brush stroke you create.

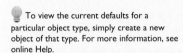

To view the current defaults for a particular object type, simply create a new object of that type. For more information, see online Help.

DrawPlus provides you with two methods of setting brush stroke (or any object) defaults:

- Update Defaults
- Synchronize Defaults

Updating defaults

Use this command to set up defaults before you create a new brush stroke.

To update brush stroke defaults

1 Create a single brush stroke and fine-tune its properties as desired—or use an existing brush stroke that already has the properties you want to use as the basis for new defaults.

2 Select the brush stroke, then right-click and select **Update Defaults** (or choose **Update Object Defaults** from the **Format** menu).

Some default settings are recorded as 'master settings,' which will be in effect the next time you start DrawPlus or create a new document. You can change which settings become master settings. For details "Recording master settings" in online Help.

Synchronizing Defaults

On the Standard toolbar the ⊞ **Synchronize Defaults** drop-down list provides three options that you can use to control the default properties of any DrawPlus object. In this section, we'll discuss how these options specifically relate to brush strokes.

Synchronize Defaults

- If this option is **selected**, any new brush
  stroke you make (or any object you
  create—a line or QuickShape for
  example) will assume the properties of
  the last stroke you created. If you change
  the properties again, those properties
  now become the new defaults and will be
  picked up by your next brush stroke.

  In addition, if you select (click on) a previously created brush stroke,
  your next stroke assumes the properties of the stroke you selected.

- If this option is **not selected**, any new brush stroke you make assumes
  the DrawPlus default properties. This means that if you want to
  continue painting with the same brush style settings, you have to reset
  the properties again for each new stroke.

Synchronization Settings

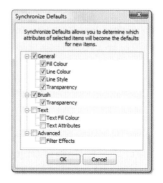

- Click this option to open the
  Synchronize Defaults dialog. Here,
  you can select which object attributes
  you want to become the new default
  properties. Any new brush stroke will
  now assume only the selected
  properties of the last stroke you
  created. If you change the properties
  again, those properties will be picked
  up by the next stroke.

  If you select a previously created
  brush stroke, your next stroke
  assumes the properties of the stroke
  you selected.

Reset Object Defaults

- If you click this option, DrawPlus will revert to the original **global**
  defaults. This means that if you've changed defaults for other objects,
  such as shapes and lines, those defaults will also be reverted.

To create brush strokes without synchronizing defaults

1   Click **Synchronize Defaults** to deselect
    it, then create a few black brush strokes on your
    page.

2   Use the **Pointer** tool to select one of the
    strokes, then on the **Swatch** tab, change the
    stroke colour to red.

3   Click the **Paintbrush** tool and paint a new
    stroke. The colour reverts to the black of your original stroke.

To synchronize brush stroke defaults

1   In the **Synchronize Defaults** drop-down list, click
    Synchronization Settings. In the dialog, in the **General** section,
    click the following properties: Fill Colour, Line Colour, Line Style, and
    Transparency.

    Now create a few black brush strokes on your page.

2   Use the **Pointer** tool to select a stroke, then on the **Swatch** tab,
    change the stroke colour to red.

3   Click the **Paintbrush** tool again
    and paint a new brush stroke. The
    new stroke picks up the red colour of
    the previous stroke.

4   Create a new stroke and apply a
    different colour.

5   Create another stroke—the stroke
    picks up the colour you chose in step
    4.

6   Using the **Paintbrush** tool, click on
    one of the red brush strokes and then
    draw a new stroke.

This stroke picks up the defaults from the stroke you just clicked, so it
will be red.

Congratulations, you've completed the tutorial! As you can see, there's a
lot you can do with the natural media brushes. (You'll find more
information in online Help.)

Using Spray Brushes

The DrawPlus X3 **Brushes** tab includes a wide selection of new spray brushes, which you can use to create some impressive artistic effects.

In this tutorial, we'll use spray brushes to create smoke, clouds, and moss effects.

You'll learn how to:

- Add layers and change layer properties.
- Draw QuickShapes.
- Apply and edit solid and gradient fills.
- Apply filter effects.
- Crop objects.
- Create and edit spray brush strokes.

Spray brush types

On the **Brushes** tab, the spray brushes are denoted with the 🖌 icon. Spray brushes can be divided into two main categories:

- Those based on *photos*—for example, the **Beads**, **Candy**, and **Confetti** brushes in the **Photo** category. You cannot recolour these brushes.

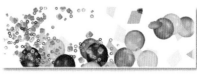

- Those based on *textures*—such as those in the **Airbrushes** and **Grunge** categories. You can recolour these brushes.

In this tutorial we'll use both types of brushes to create the image illustrated on the right.

Setting up the document

We'll start with a new blank document, and then add some new layers.

To open a new blank document:

1   From the Startup Wizard, click **Create > Start New Drawing**.

2   In the **Start From Scratch** dialog, choose the page size of your choice and click **Open**.

3   On the Standard toolbar, click  **Save**.

4   Save your file as Cloudy Night.dpp.

Our new document comprises a single layer, displayed on the **Layers** tab, and named **Layer 1**.

We could create our image on this layer. However, for best practice, we'll add each element to a new layer. We'll add these layers now, naming them appropriately as we go.

To rename a layer:

1   Double-click on Layer 1 to open the **Layer Properties** dialog.

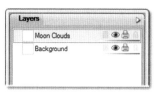

2   Name the layer 'Background' and click **OK**.

To add new layers:

1   On the **Layers** tab, click  **Add Layer**.

DrawPlus adds a new layer above the Background layer, naming it 'Layer 1.'

2   Double-click on the new Layer 1.

3   In the **Layer Properties** dialog, rename the layer 'Moon Clouds' and click **OK**.

4   Repeat steps 1 to 3 to add three more layers.

Name these layers 'Moon,' 'Trees,' and 'Bird' respectively.

When you've finished, the **Layers** tab should look like the one illustrated here.

If your layers are not stacked in the same order as ours, move them by clicking and dragging them to the desired position in the stack.

Adding shapes, images, fills, and effects

We'll now create the dark sky and 'glowing' moon.

To create the dark sky:

1   On the **Layers** tab, click on the **Background** layer to make it the active layer (the active layer is shown with blue highlighting).

2   On the Drawing toolbar, on the ☐▾ QuickShapes flyout, click the **Quick Rectangle**.

3   Click and drag to draw a rectangle to fill the page.

4   Select the rectangle and then open the **Swatch** tab.

• Expand the ☐▾ **Gradient** drop-down list and click **Linear**.

• Click the **Linear 11** swatch to apply it to the shape.

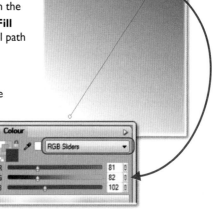

5   With the shape still selected, on the Drawing toolbar, click the ◈ **Fill Tool**. This displays the linear fill path and its nodes.

6   On the **Colour** tab:

• Select **RGB Sliders** from the drop-down list.

• Click the top fill path node enter RGB values of 81, 82, and 102.

- Click the bottom node and enter RGB values of 11, 12, and 29.

7 Click and drag the fill path nodes so that the angle of the fill path is the same as our example, illustrated on the right.

(To provide a clearer illustration, we've enlarged the fill path nodes in this example.)

That's it, the first layer is complete!

Let's work on the **Moon** layer next.

To add the glowing moon:

1 On the **Layers** tab, click on the **Moon** layer to make it the active layer.

2 On the Drawing toolbar, click  **Insert Picture**. In the **Open** dialog, browse to your **...Tutorials\Workspace** folder, select the **Moon.jpg** file and click **Open**.

In a default installation, you'll find the **Workspace** folder in the following location:

C:\Program Files\Serif\DrawPlus\X3\Tutorials\Workspace

3 Click and drag on the page to insert the image in the upper right corner.

4 On the Drawing toolbar, on the QuickShapes flyout, click the **Quick Ellipse**.

5 In the upper-left corner of the **Swatch** tab, click the Fill swatch and then on the palette, click **None**.

6   Press and hold down the **Shift** key,
    and then click and drag to draw an
    ellipse roughly the same size as the
    moon.

    Drag the shape so that it sits directly
    on top of the moon. Resize it to fit by
    dragging a corner resize handle.

7   With the shape still selected, hold
    down the **Shift** key and then click on
    the black background area of the
    imported image.

    Now both the shape and the image are selected.

8   On the **Arrange** tab, in the
    Crop/Clip drop-down list, click
    Crop to Top Object.

    The image background is cropped,
    leaving just the moon on the page.

    We have our basic moon, now let's
    apply some filter effects to make it
    glow.

9   With the moon selected, on the
    Drawing toolbar, click 🌟 **Filter
    Effects**.

10 In the **Filter Effects**
    dialog, select the **Outer
    Glow** check box and set
    the following values.

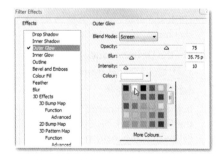

    • **Blend Mode**: Screen

    • **Opacity:** 75

    • **Blur:** 35.75

    • **Intensity**: 10

    • **Colour:** White

11 Select the **Inner Glow** check box and set the following values.

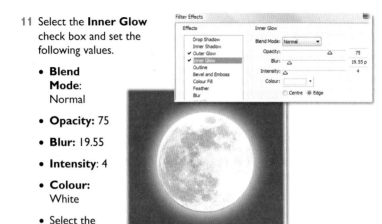

- **Blend Mode**: Normal

- **Opacity:** 75

- **Blur:** 19.55

- **Intensity**: 4

- **Colour:** White

- Select the **Edge** option.

Using the spray brushes

In the following sections, we'll use a selection of spray brushes to add clouds and trees to our image.

To add the clouds:

1 On the **Layers** tab, click on the **Moon Clouds** layer to make it the active layer.

2 On the Drawing toolbar, click the 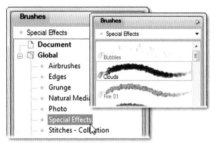 **Paintbrush Tool**.

3 On the **Brushes** tab, in the drop-down brush category list, select **Special Effects**.

Select the **Clouds** brush.

4 To set the brush stroke colour, open the **Swatch** tab and click a light grey swatch.

5   At the top of the workspace, on the Brush context toolbar, set the
    brush **Width** to 60 pt and the **Opacity** to 40%.

6   Now click and drag to paint some
    clouds around the edge of the moon.

7   Continue building up the cloud area
    until you've achieved the effect you
    want.

For the best results, vary
the brush colour, width,
and opacity.

To add the trees:

1   On the **Layers** tab, click on the **Trees** layer to make it the active
    layer.

2   On the **Brushes** tab, in
    the **Special Effects**
    category, select the **Moss**
    brush.

3   On the context toolbar,
    set a large brush width.

4   Click and drag in the
    lower section of your page
    to create the treetops.

    For the best results, vary
    the brush width and
    opacity.

    Note: You can't adjust
    the colour of this photo-
    based spray brush.

You can edit the properties of brush strokes that you've already added to your page.

To edit a brush stroke:

1 Select the stroke with the **Paintbrush Tool**.

2 Adjust the settings on the Brush context toolbar and **Swatch** tab.

3 The stroke updates automatically on the page.

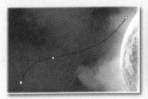 

Adding the bird silhouette

With our clouds and trees in place, we're ready to add the bird silhouette.

To add the bird silhouette:

1 On the **Layers** tab, click on the **Bird** layer to make it the active layer.

2 On the **File** menu, click **Open**.

 To create a silhouette from one of your own photos, you could use the DrawPlus Cutout Studio to first remove the subject of a photo from its background, or you could use the Line tools to trace around your subject.

If you'd like to try these methods for yourself, see the following tutorials:

Brushes & Art: Cutting Out and Tracing Images

Mastering the Basics: Working with Line Tools

3 Browse to your **Workspace** folder (by default **C:\Program Files\Serif\DrawPlus\X3\Tutorials\Workspace**) and open the **Silhouette.dpp** file.

4 Right-click the silhouette you want to use in your image and click **Copy**. Close the Silhouette.dpp file.

5 Back in the Cloudy Night.dpp file, right-click on the page and click **Paste**.

6 Drag the pasted silhouette into position, resizing it as required.

7   With the silhouette selected, open
    the **Colour** tab.

For both the Line and Fill swatches,
set all three of the RGB
values to 51.

This softens the silhouette
and produces a more
realistic effect.

If you've followed all of the
steps in this tutorial, you
should now have an image that
resembles ours.

We hope you've enjoyed
working with the spray
brushes, along with the other
DrawPlus features we've
explored here.

We look forward to seeing
your spray brush creations on
the www.DrawPlus.com
website!

For information on the
www.drawplus.com website, and
instructions on how to register
and upload your designs, see
online Help.

Using Pressure Sensitivity

All of the brushes within DrawPlus are pressure sensitive, allowing you to create realistic-looking brush strokes when using a graphics tablet. However, the **Pressure** tab allows you to re-create the same effect regardless of whether you have a tablet.

In this tutorial, you'll learn how to:

- Adjust the pressure-sensitivity and pressure profile of your brush strokes.

- Create and save your own pressure profiles.

The Pressure tab

When you work with paint, pencil, charcoal, or any other type of natural medium, you can dramatically change the appearance of your strokes by varying the pressure with which you apply the medium to the paper or canvas.

With DrawPlus, you can achieve the same flexibility in the following ways:

- By using a pressure-sensitive pen and tablet and varying pressure just as you would with a 'real' pencil or pen.

- By using the **Pressure** tab to adjust the pressure of strokes made with a pen and tablet and with a mouse. Note that you can also use this method to change the pressure of **previously created** strokes.

To see how you can control pressure-sensitivity using the **Pressure** tab, follow the procedure outlined below.

To adjust pressure-sensitivity

1   Click the 🖌 **Paintbrush** tool, then on the
    Brushes tab select a stroke style of
    your choice and draw a line on the
    page.

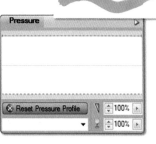

2   With the brush stroke selected, click
    the **Pressure** tab (you may need to
    expand it—click the ▷ **Tab Menu**
    and then click **Expand**).

    By default, this new brush stroke will
    have no pressure profile selected.

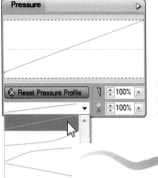

3   Click to expand the Pressure Profile
    drop-down list, and then click to
    select the first profile in the list.

    The appearance of your brush stroke
    changes to reflect the new profile.

Note how the intensity of the brush
stroke changes to correspond with the
change in pressure, varying from no
pressure at the start of the stroke
to maximum pressure at the end
of the stroke.

⚠ When working with a pen and pressure-sensitive tablet, you can only apply a pressure profile to strokes you have previously created. By default, as you create a new stroke, pressure applied with the pen will override the pressure profile set on the **Pressure** tab.

4   In the Pressure Profile drop-down list, select some different profiles and note how they affect the appearance of your brush stroke.

💡 To remove a selected pressure profile and return to the default setting, click **Reset Pressure Profile**.

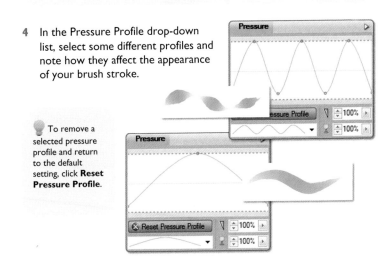

As you can see, DrawPlus provides you with a range of preset pressure profiles from which to choose. However, you can also edit a profile and, if you wish, save it for use in future documents. Let's see how this is done...

To edit and save a new pressure profile

1   On the **Pressure** tab, choose any preset pressure profile from the list.

2   In the profile display pane, click a point on the blue profile line and drag to a new position.

A node is created at the new point— you can create as many of these nodes as you wish. After creating the nodes, you can move them or delete them as required:

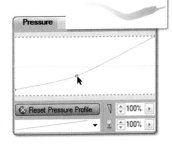

- To move a node, simply click and drag it.

- To delete a node, select it and then press **Delete**.

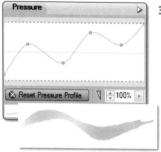

3 When you are happy with your pressure profile, click the ▷ **Tab Menu** in the upper right corner of the tab and select **Add Pressure Profile**.

Your new profile is added to the preset pressure profiles in the drop-down list.

Adjusting pressure variance

The dotted lines at the upper and lower edges of the profile display pane indicate the **range of variance** of the pressure profile. You can move these lines to limit the **maximum** and **minimum** pressure you want to apply with a brush stroke.

This feature is particularly useful if you are using a mouse, since the mouse does not have the pressure-sensitivity of a pen and tablet.

Example 1

Here, the maximum and minimum pressure values have not been adjusted, so the brush stroke pressure range is not limited.

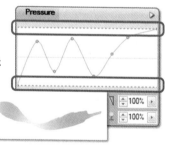

Example 2

In this example, we **decreased the maximum pressure** value of the stroke by moving the upper line down.

Compared to Example 1, this brush stroke appears much less intense at its 'peak' points.

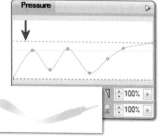

Example 3

Here we **increased the minimum pressure** value of the stroke by moving the lower line up.

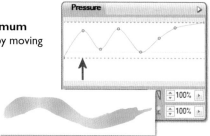

Compared to Example 1, this brush stroke appears more intense at its 'trough' points.

As you can see, even if you do not have access to a pressure-sensitive pen and tablet, you can still produce realistic pressure variance with a mouse by simply adjusting the pressure profile of your brush strokes.

Adjusting brush stroke thickness and transparency

Now let's look at the two controls in the lower right corner of the **Pressure** tab: **Thickness** and **Transparency**. Displayed as percentages, these values affect how the width and transparency of a brush stroke change as its pressure changes.

For example, suppose you are painting with a 'real' paintbrush... As you apply more pressure with the brush, the mark you make on the page becomes thicker and more dense (opaque). With DrawPlus, you can achieve the same effect. However, you can also limit how much the thickness and transparency will vary along the length of a particular brush stroke by adjusting these percentage values.

If you're having difficulty imagining this, the following examples should help.

Example 1

Thickness: 100%

Transparency: 100%

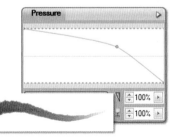

Here, we are allowing the maximum amount of variance along the length of the stroke.

As the stroke pressure decreases, note how the thickness decreases and the transparency increases correspondingly.

Example 2

Thickness: 0%

Transparency: 100%

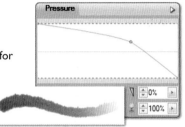

We are allowing maximum variance for transparency, but no variance for thickness.

As the pressure decreases, the stroke becomes more transparent but the width of the stroke remains constant.

Example 3

Thickness: 100%

Transparency: 0%

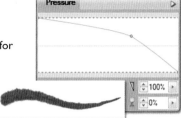

We are allowing maximum variance for thickness, but no variance for transparency.

As the pressure decreases, the stroke becomes thinner but the transparency does not change.

Example 4

Thickness: 0%

Transparency: 0%

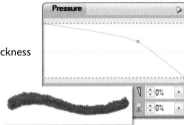

We are allowing no variance for thickness or transparency .

As the pressure decreases, there is no change in either the width or transparency of the brush stroke.

Example 5

Thickness: 50%

Transparency: 50%

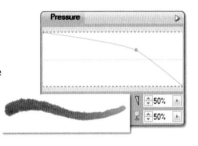

We are allowing 50% variance for thickness and transparency.

As the pressure decreases, both the width and transparency of the brush stroke change. However, because we have limited the range of variance to 50% of the maximum, the end of the brush stroke is thicker and less transparent than in Example 1.

We suggest that you experiment with these settings yourself to see the different effects you can achieve.

Cutting Out
and Tracing Images

DrawPlus includes the following dedicated studio environments:

Cutout Studio—which allows you to separate the subject of a photo from its background.

AutoTrace Studio—which lets you trace imported images and convert them to vector objects. You can then manipulate the traced output by adjusting nodes and curves, editing colour fills, and merging areas.

In this tutorial, we'll use these two environments to produce a contemporary design effect, similar to that created by the artist Jason Brooks.

You'll learn how to:

- Use Cutout Studio to separate the subject of the photo from its background.

- Use AutoTrace Studio to create a colour tracing of the subject.

- Create a custom autotrace profile.

- Place the completed traced output onto a new background.

You'll find the photograph used in this tutorial in your **Workspace** folder. In a default installation, this folder is installed to the following location:

C:\Program Files\Serif\DrawPlus\X3\Tutorials\Workspace

Cutting out the image

To begin, we'll use Cutout Studio to separate the subject of our photo from its background.

To cut out the image:

1   Open DrawPlus. In the Startup Wizard, click **Start New Drawing**.

2   Choose an **A4** or **Letter** page size, in **Portrait** orientation, and click **OK**.

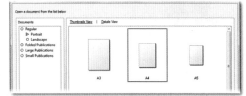

3   On the Drawing toolbar, click 🖻 **Insert Picture**, browse to your **Tutorials\Workspace** folder and open the **Grunge Girl.jpg** file.

4   Resize the image so that if fills the page.

5   Select the image, and then on the Picture context toolbar, click 🖋 Cutout Studio . The image opens in the Cutout Studio window.

6   On the left toolbar, click the 🖌 **Discard Brush Tool**.

7   On the horizontal toolbar, click to select the ⊘ **Large Brush**.

8   Click and drag on the image background to mark the areas you want to discard.

As you do so, DrawPlus locates similar adjoining areas and extends your selection to incorporate them.

9   In the lower-right corner of the window, on the View toolbar:

   • Click the 🔍 **Zoom In** button (or drag the zoom slider to the right) to zoom into the image.

   • Click the ✋ **Pan** tool and then drag on the image, positioning it so that you can work on the area surrounding the subject's head.

> 💡 To temporarily switch to the **Pan** tool, press the spacebar.
>
> When you have finished panning your image, revert to the Brush tool you were last using, by pressing the spacebar again.

10 Click the ▦ **Discard Brush Tool**, (or press the spacebar), and then on the horizontal toolbar, click the 🖌 **Small Brush**.

11 Click, or click and drag, on the image to remove the smaller background areas around the subject's head and arms.

   Note: If you inadvertently select an area that you don't want to discard, you can click ↶ Undo to undo your previous step(s).

   However, don't worry if some small areas of the image are marked as discarded. This will occur because some of colours present

on the subject are similar to the background colour. We can easily correct this using the 🖌 **Keep Brush Tool**.

Before we do so, let's first change the colour of the 'discarded' and 'kept' areas of the image. This will make it easier to identify any discarded areas that we need to 'add' back to our subject.

12 On the left toolbar, click ▦ **Show Tinted**.

13 Click the **Keep Brush Tool**.

14 On the horizontal toolbar, reduce the **Grow Tolerance** value to **10**.

15 Using a small brush size, click and drag on any discarded areas that you want to keep.

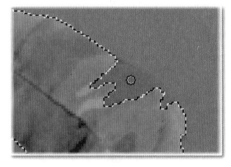

> **Grow Tolerance**
>
> This setting controls the amount by which the area under the cursor is expanded (by detecting colours similar to those within the current selection). The higher the value the more the selected area will 'grow.'
>
> Generally, use higher **Grow Tolerance** values when selecting large areas; use lower values when working on more intricate details of an image.

Note: If you inadvertently 'keep' some areas that you want to discard, you can switch back to the **Discard Brush Tool** and then reselect these areas.

16 Click [⊙ Preview] to preview your cutout area on a transparent background.

17 Optional: In Preview mode, you can use the ✎ **Restore Touch-up** and ▥ **Erase Touch-up** tools to further refine the cutout. (

For instructions, see "*Step 4: Refining and completing the cutout*," in the Cutout Studio **Help** pane.)

18 When you are happy with your image, click [✓ OK] to proceed with the cutout and return to the DrawPlus workspace.

Tracing the image

We'll now use AutoTrace Studio to trace around the cutout image and convert it to a vector graphic.

To trace the image:

1 Select the image and on the Picture context toolbar, click [AutoTrace ▾].

2 In the AutoTrace Studio Startup Wizard, click **Photo Image Trace**.

   The image opens in the AutoTrace Studio environment.

3 At the right of the workspace, you'll see a range of control sliders.

   Usually, you'll want to experiment with these until you achieve the desired effect. For the purpose of this tutorial, drag the sliders to set the following values:

   We suggest you return to AutoTrace Studio later and experiment with the settings. Different values can produce quite different results. (For details, see the AutoTrace Studio **Help** pane.)

   Smoothing Filter: 0

   Flatten: 21

   Curve Smoothing Filter: 0

   Resample Scale: 100%

   Minimum Area: 10pix

   Curve Optimization: 10

   Thickness Tolerance 11

   Sharp Edge Tolerance: 72

4 Click [Trace] to create the tracing.

   You can save your autotrace settings to a custom profile, allowing you to quickly apply the same settings to multiple images.

   To save a custom profile:

   1 In the upper-right corner of AutoTrace Studio, click
      Save Current Profile.

   2 In the **Save Profile** dialog, type a name for your profile and click **OK**.

   Your custom profile appears in the profile drop-down list.

Our initial traced output looks pretty good, but we can improve it. In the following section, we'll adjust and refine the image tracing using the **Merge**, **Fill**, and **Node** tools.

To merge areas:

1   In the lower-right corner of the dialog, click .

Using the 📷 **Zoom In** and 🖐 **Pan** tools, position the image so that you can work on the girl's face and head.

You'll see that the face is comprised of several different coloured areas. We don't need all of these skin tone variations so we'll merge some of them.

2   On the horizontal toolbar, click 🖌 Merge Tool.

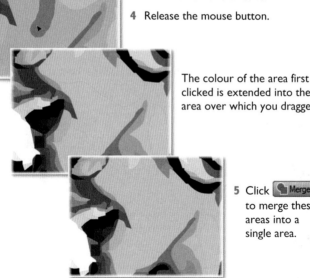

3   Click on the lighter area of the upper cheek, and then drag down, passing over the darker skin tone.

4   Release the mouse button.

The colour of the area first clicked is extended into the area over which you dragged.

5   Click 🐾 Merge to merge these areas into a single area.

💡 When merging smaller areas, you will need to reduce the brush size.

6   Repeat steps 3 to 5 to merge other areas of the image, zooming out of
    the image periodically to check your
    results.

For example, we merged:

• The lips, and the shadowed areas of
  the chin and neck.

  • The upper
    cheek, headphones, and stomach area.

We'll now use the 🪣 Fill Tool to 'paint' the
stomach area with the slightly darker skin
tone used on the face.

To fill an area:

1   Zoom into the face and then, on the horizontal toolbar, click 🪣 Fill Tool.

2   To the right of the preview window, you'll see the **Palette** controls.
    Click on a blank palette swatch and then click the 🖊 **Colour
    Selector**.

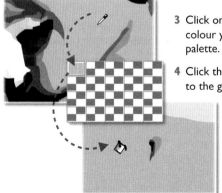

3   Click on the main part of the face. The
    colour you clicked is added to the
    palette.

4   Click the ✋ **Pan Tool** and pan down
    to the girls' stomach.

5   Click the 🪣 Fill Tool, click
    your new palette swatch,
    and then click on the main
    stomach area to fill it with
    the palette colour.

As you work on your image, you'll notice that some areas (such as the chin and lips) could be further improved by reshaping. We can use the **Node tools** for this...

To adjust nodes:

1   Zoom into the area you want to reshape, and then, on the horizontal toolbar, click ![Node Tool].

2   At the right of the workspace, click the ![icon] **Select Tool**.

3   Click on the leftmost part of the lip to display its nodes and curve segments.

4   There are various ways to reshape a selected area.

For example, you can:

- Click and drag the nodes (indicated with small squares around the border of the selected area).

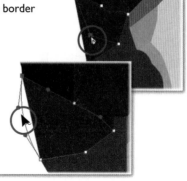

- Click and drag the curve segments (the lines that connect nodes).

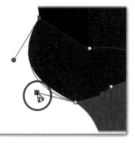

- Click and drag the curve control handles (displayed as blue circles on either side of a selected node).

- To add a new node, simply click on a curve segment, at the point where you want to add the new node.

![icon] For more information on working with the Node tools, see the AutoTrace **Help** tab.

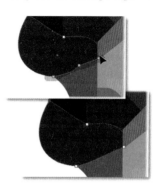

- To smooth out nodes, click the **Smooth Tool**, then click and drag over the nodes you want to smooth.

- To erase nodes, click the **Erase Tool** and then click and drag over the nodes you want to erase.

To complete the tracing:

- If you are happy with the image, click **Accept** to complete the tracing and return to the DrawPlus workspace.

To fine-tune settings:

1 Click **Back**.

2 Adjust the settings as required and click **Trace**.

3 Optional: Click **Adjust** to make further adjustments using the **Merge**, **Fill**, and **Node** tools.

4 Click **Accept**.

Creating the new image background

To complete this project, we'll create a new background for our traced image. We'll add two new layers to the document—Background and Strobes—and we'll work with QuickShapes, fills, and filter effects.

To create the Background layer:

1 On the **Layers** tab, you'll see your traced image on Layer I.

Click **Add Layer** to add a new layer.

2 Click on Layer I, and then drag it up above Layer 2.

3 Make Layer 2 the *active layer* by selecting it on the tab. (The active layer is highlighted in blue.)

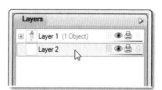

4   On the Drawing toolbar, on the
    QuickShapes flyout, click the
    Quick Rectangle.

    Click and drag to draw a rectangle
    that completely fills the page.

5   With the rectangle selected:

    • Open the **Swatch** tab, expand the
      Gradient drop-down list and
      click **Four Colour**.

    • Click the **Linear Four Colour 70**
      swatch to apply it to the shape.

6   On the **Layers** tab, double-click on Layer 2 to open the **Layer
    Properties** dialog. In the **Name** box, type 'Background.' Click **OK**.

To create the Strobes layer:

1   Click ⊞ **Add Layer** to add a third layer. Repeat step 6 in the
    previous section, naming this new layer 'Strobes.'

2   Click the ● **Visible** button next to Layer 1 to temporarily hide the
    photo.

    Ensure that the **Strobes**
    layer sits above the
    Background layer and is
    the active layer.

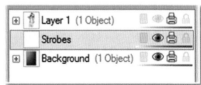

3   On the QuickShapes flyout, click the ☆ **Quick Star**, and then click and drag to draw a large star in the middle of the page.

4   With the star selected, open the **Swatch** tab:

   • Expand the 🎨▾ **Palettes** drop-down list and click **Standard RGB**.

   • Click the **Fill** swatch, and then click the white colour swatch to apply it to the star.

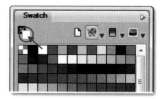

5   On the Drawing toolbar, click the ▽ **Node Tool**.

   Four nodes display around the outside of the star.

   • Drag the top node to the right, increasing the number of points to 12.

   • Drag the left node down, increasing the inner radius to 117.5 pix. (If your ruler units are set to centimetres, set this value to 3.11 cm.)

   🔍 To change your ruler units, click **Tools > Options**, and then select the **Layout** option.

6   With the shape selected, open the **Colour** tab and drag the **Opacity** slider to set the value to 33%.

7   On the Drawing toolbar, click 🌟 **Filter Effects**.

8   In the **Filter Effects** dialog:

   • Select the **Feather** effect check box and set the **Blur** value to 7.5 pt.

   • Select the **Blur** effect check box, select the **Gaussian** blur type and set the **Blur** value to 10.5 pt.

   • Click **OK**.

9   Now let's copy the shape: With the 🔍 **Pointer Tool**, right-click the shape and click **Copy**. Right-click again and click **Paste**.

10   A copy of the shape is pasted on top of the original and selected.

   Hold down the **Shift** key and click once on the shapes. Now both shapes are selected.

11 To centre the selected shapes, open the **Align** tab:

- Click 🖼 **Horizontal Centre**.
- Click 📊 **Vertical Centre**.

12 Click away from the shapes to deselect them both. Now click once on the shapes to select just one of them.

13 To rotate the selected shape, open the **Transform** tab and in the **Rotation** box, enter 345°.

(To do this, you can use the arrow keys; click the right arrow and drag the slider; or type 345 and then press the **Enter** key.)

14 To resize the shape, press and hold down the **Ctrl** key, and then click and drag a corner resize handle outwards.

15 To see the results of all your hard work:

On the Layers tab, click the 👁 **Visible** button next to Layer 1 to redisplay the photo.

💡 When the photo is placed on top of the new coloured background, you may see small areas of the original background that were not removed in Cutout Studio.

To delete background areas:

1 On the **Layers** tab, select the layer containing the photo.

2 On your page, right-click the photo and click **Ungroup**.

3 Select the area you want to remove and press the **Delete** key.

To regroup the photo elements:

1 On the **Edit** menu, click **Select All** (or press **Ctrl + A**) to select all of the elements.

2 Right-click the selection and click **Group**.

In this tutorial, we've introduced you to some very powerful tools. We hope you'll continue to experiment and have fun creating cutouts and tracings of your own images.

Why not upload your creations to the www.DrawPlus.com website! For details, see 'Sharing via website' in the DrawPlus online Help.

Turning Photos into Art

The DrawPlus **Brushes** tab contains a vast array of pressure-sensitive brush strokes. These powerful tools emulate traditional 'natural media' effects, providing you with a realistic painting or drawing experience. You'll be excited by the possibilities open to you—create pencil sketches, charcoal drawings, watercolours, and oil paintings. You can even experiment with a combination of media effects. The only thing limiting you is your imagination...

In this tutorial, we'll show you how to:

Adjust the pressure sensitivity of your Serif GraphicsPad pen and tablet.

- Build up a composition using layers.
- Apply brush strokes (using either the mouse or a pen and tablet).
- Turn a landscape photograph into a watercolour painting.
- Turn a portrait photograph into a charcoal sketch.

> If you have not yet worked with the **Brushes** tab and its associated controls, we suggest you complete the *Using the Natural Media Brushes* tutorial before beginning this one.

Adjusting the pressure sensitivity of the GraphicsPad pen and tablet

We'll start this tutorial by showing you how to customize the **pressure sensitivity** of your Serif GraphicsPad pen and tablet using the **Tablet Properties** dialog. (If you're unfamiliar with the term, pressure sensitivity refers to the amount of pressure needed to click or draw with the pen.)

The **Tablet Properties** dialog contains various other settings that control the behaviour of your pen and tablet. In this section, we'll focus on pressure sensitivity alone; however, we suggest you experiment with all of the settings to discover what works best for you.

This section assumes that you have already installed your Serif GraphicsPad.

For information about installation and setup procedures, refer to the *Serif GraphicsPad User Manual* and tutorials.

Similarly, if you are using a different pen and tablet, refer to the accompanying documentation.

To adjust pressure sensitivity

1   Open the GraphicsPad **Tablet Properties** dialog. You can do this in one of the following ways:

   - On the system taskbar, double-click the GraphicsPad icon, or right-click it and choose **Tablet Properties**.

   - Double-click the GraphicsPad desktop shortcut that was created when you installed the tablet software.

   - Click the Windows **Start** button, choose **All Programs** (for versions other than Windows XP, choose the **Programs** group), choose **Tablet**, then click **Tablet Properties**.

2 In the dialog, drag the slider to achieve a softer or firmer setting. In general:

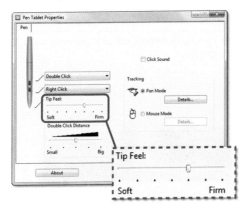

- Use a firm tip setting when you want maximum control. For example, when drawing thin lines and strokes.

- Use a soft tip setting when you want to create broad strokes, or when a wider range of pressure values is required.

For details on this and other settings, see the Serif GraphicsPad User Manual.

When you're happy with your pen and tablet settings, you're ready to open DrawPlus and start painting. Let's begin with a watercolour...

💡 The watercolour and portrait files that were created for this tutorial, and the original source images, are provided in your **...\Workspace** folder. In a standard installation, you'll find this folder in the following location:

C:\Program Files\Serif\DrawPlus\X3\Tutorials

The **Watercolour.dpp** and **Portrait.dpp** files each comprise multiple pages, which you can click through to see how we built up the final image.

We've also included 📝 **PageHints** to help explain key elements—simply double-click a PageHint icon to open its dialog.

The DrawPlus **Samples** collection also includes the final watercolour and portrait images. To open a sample, in the DrawPlus Startup Wizard, click **View Samples** and then browse to locate the file you want to open.

Example 1: Create a landscape in watercolours

If you love the look of traditional watercolour paintings, you'll be delighted with the DrawPlus watercolour brushes. In this exercise, we'll show you to turn a landscape photograph into a delicate watercolour composition.

1   In the DrawPlus Startup Wizard, choose **Drawing**, select a Letter or A4 Landscape page size and click **Open**.

2   On the Drawing toolbar, click the  **Insert Picture** button, browse to your **Workspace** folder and open the **Landscape.jpg** file.

Resize and position the image so that it takes up most of the page, as illustrated.

3   Over on the **Layers** tab, you'll see that your document currently contains a single layer—**Layer 1**, containing the photograph.

As we build up our watercolour image, we'll create additional layers for each of the elements of the composition. To begin, let's add a layer for the background—in this case, the sky.

To create the background

1   On the **Layers** tab, click the ➕ **Add Layer** button. Right-click the new layer—**Layer 2**— and click **Layer Properties**.

In the **Layer Properties** dialog, in the **Name** box, type a new name for the layer—e.g., 'Sky' or 'Background,' and click **OK**.

2   On the Drawing toolbar, on the Quick Shapes flyout, click the ▭ **Quick Rectangle** and draw a rectangle the same size as your image. Move the shape down, so that you can see the sky in the original photograph.

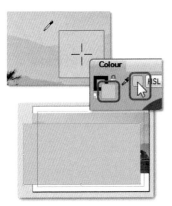

3   On the **Colour** tab, click and drag the 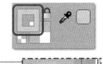 **Colour Picker** to select a colour from the sky.

4   Click to select the **Fill** swatch and then double-click the **Picked Colour** swatch. The fill is applied to the shape.

5   On the **Line** tab, remove the shape's outline by clicking ⊞ **None**.

Next, we're going to add some realistic looking paintbrush strokes to the base colour of the sky.

6   Click the 🔧 **Pointer** tool and then click in the workspace area. The rectangle will be deselected.

7   On the Drawing toolbar, click the 🖌 **Paintbrush** tool.

8   On the **Brushes** tab, in the category drop-down list, choose **Natural Media** and select one of the **Watery Paint** brushes.

9   On the Brush context toolbar, change to a wide brush stroke by increasing the **Width** value.

10 On the **Colour** tab, use the 🖊 **Colour Picker** to select a slightly lighter colour for the sky. To apply the colour to the line, click to select the **Line** swatch and then double-click the **Picked Colour** swatch.

11 Paint over the rectangle using broad, sweeping strokes. Don't worry about painting over the edges of the rectangle—we'll tidy up next.

💡 When making long, sweeping strokes, you'll get the best results if you choose a **repeating brush**.

To check if a brush stroke is repeating or non-repeating, right-click it on the **Brushes** tab and select **Edit**.

In the **Body repeat method** box, non-repeating brushes are assigned a **None - Stretch** value; repeating brushes are assigned any other value.

12 On the **Edit** menu, click Select All.

On the **Arrange** tab, click to expand the 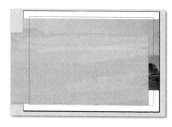 **Crop/Clip** flyout and then, click **Clip to Bottom object**.

The ends of the brush strokes are clipped to the border of the rectangle.

13 Move the shape off the page for now, so that you can see the photograph.

14 On the Drawing toolbar, click the 🖊 **Pen** tool, then click to trace around the outline of the hills in the distance.

- Apply a fill to the shape (you'll need to click the **Fill** button in the top left corner of the **Swatch** or **Colour** tab first).

- Remove its outline.

- Paint over it using broad brush strokes.

As with all brush strokes, the appearance of a watercolour stroke remains adjustable, even after you have moved on to other areas of your painting. You'll find this invaluable as it allows you to experiment with the look of your painting.

To adjust the properties of a brush stroke, use the controls on the **Brush context toolbar**. For details, see online Help or the *Using the Natural Media Brushes* tutorial.

15 Use the 🔍 **Pointer** tool to draw a selection bounding box around the shape and all the brush strokes.

On the 🔲, **Crop/Clip** flyout, click **Clip to Bottom**.

DrawPlus clips the ends of the brush strokes to the border of the shape behind it.

16 Repeat this procedure to trace around all of the objects in the background of the photo.

To create the foreground

1 On the **Layers** tab, click the ➕ **Add Layer** button to create a third layer. Name this layer 'Hills.'

On the **Hills** layer, use the technique described previously to create the green hills.

2 Add another layer and rename it 'Grass.' Use this layer to create the bright green grass section in the foreground.

We're now ready to move on to the detail of our image.

To add the foreground detail

1   Add a fourth layer and rename it 'Trees.' Use this layer to 'block in' the shapes of the trees and some of the larger foreground areas. Use varying brush widths and strokes to create background shapes on which to add the detail later.

2   Add another layer and rename it 'Tree Detail.' On this layer, use a small brush width to paint in the branches and other details of the trees.

It will help if you zoom into the composition to trace over these detailed areas.

3   To complete the watercolour, add two more layers—'Foreground Trees' and 'Foreground Detail.' Again, choose a small brush and zoom into the areas you want to trace.

💡 To see the various background elements we created, see pages 1 and 2 of the sample file, **Watercolour.dpp**.

For the hills and grass composition, see page 3.

Here, we've hidden the **Sky**, **Hills**, **Grass**, and **Trees** layers so that you can see exactly what we painted on our **Tree Detail** layer.

As you are building up your composition, it might help you to focus in on an area if you hide the layers behind the one you are working on. To do this, simply click the  **Hide/Show Layer** button for the layers you want to hide.

4 When you are happy with your painting, you can delete **Layer 1**—the layer containing your original image.

To do this, on the **Layers** tab, simply select the layer to delete and then click the ⊟ **Delete** button.

That's it! Your watercolour is complete.

Example 2: Create a portrait in pastels

In this exercise, we'll show you how to turn a portrait photograph into a pastel sketch. Again, you can use our sample file, **Portrait.jpg**, which you'll find in your **Workspace** folder, or you can use one of your own photographs.

For this composition, we used some of the same techniques used in the previous example. In these cases, we have summarized the process rather than repeating it step-by-step.

1   In the DrawPlus Startup Wizard, choose **Drawing**, select a Letter or A4 Portrait page size and click **Open**.

2   On the Drawing toolbar, click the  **Insert Picture** button, browse to your **Workspace** folder and open the **Portrait.jpg** file (or choose your own image file).

Resize and position the image so that it takes up most of the page.

As we did for our watercolour, we'll create additional layers, slowly building up areas of dark, light, and mid-tones. Finally, we'll add areas of detail such as the eyes and hair. To begin, we'll add a layer for the background.

3   On the **Layers** tab, click the ⊹ **Add Layer** button. Name this layer 'Main Background.' Draw a Quick Rectangle the size of the image and apply a rich brown fill to match the background colour.

4   Add another layer and name it 'Backdrop.' On this layer, use a similar brown colour with a medium sized pastel brush (we used 41 pt), to roughly sketch in some texture to the background.

5 Create another layer and name it 'Skin.' Hide the **Backdrop** layer and, using the original image as reference, choose a smaller width pastel brush (we used 35 pt) to start adding areas of skin tone.

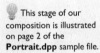 This stage of our composition is illustrated on page 2 of the **Portrait.dpp** sample file.

6 Continue to build up areas of highlights and shadows, creating new layers as you work.

Try to keep all brush strokes fluid and loose.

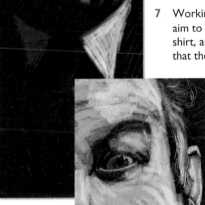

7 Working with smaller brush strokes, aim to bring out details of the suit, shirt, and tie. However, don't forget that the focus remains on the face.

With final details added—the eyes and wisps of hair—our portrait is complete! (Don't forget to delete the layer containing your original photo!)

In this exercise, we have created two very different styles of painting, using various techniques. Perhaps the most important tip to note is the extensive use of layers in both examples. Using layers like this helps you to slowly build up your image—giving you greater control over the final result.

We hope you've enjoyed this tutorial and are happy with your creations. If you're not, don't be disheartened. As with natural media techniques, painting and sketching with DrawPlus brushes takes time and practice. The more you experiment, the more proficient you will become.

Animation & Web

Varying in complexity from beginner to advanced level, these exercises let you work with keyframe animation techniques, and create website content.

Creating
Web Button Rollovers

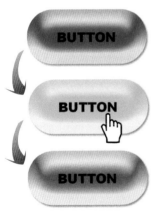

When you point to a web page graphic, your mouse pointer physically enters the screen region occupied by the graphic. You might click then on the graphic, or move the mouse out of the button region.

Underlying code can detect any of these mouse events and cause a new graphic to be swapped into the same region. In this way, a button graphic that normally appears 'up' might instantly change to 'down' when the mouse rolls over it.

In DrawPlus, it's easy to define multiple 'rollover states' for a web graphic; the necessary JavaScript code is generated automatically. In this tutorial you'll see just how easy it can be.

In this exercise, you'll learn how to:

- Set up page dimensions and ruler units.
- Add filter effects to QuickShapes.
- Create slice objects and set their properties.
- Preview your finished web button in a web browser.
- Export your web button and its rollover states.

1 In the DrawPlus Startup Wizard, choose **Drawing**, select any page size of your choice and click **Open**.

Next we'll switch to pixel-based ruler units, and trim the page area.

2 On the **Tools** menu, click **Options**.

3 In the **Options** dialog, click the **Layout** option, set the **Ruler Units** to 'pixels' and click **OK**.

4 On the **File** menu, click **Page Setup**.

5 In the **Page Setup** dialog, in the **Document Size** section, set the **Width** to 760 and the **Height** to 420. Click **OK**.

Now we'll create a button.

6 On the left Drawing toolbar, on the QuickShapes flyout, select the 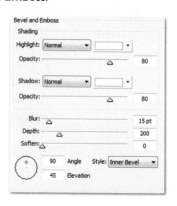 **Quick Rectangle**. Drag out a rectangle roughly 120 pixels wide by 50 high.

7 Drag the shape's slider to the top to create a round-edged lozenge shape.

8 On the **Swatch** tab, apply any solid colour fill.

9 On the **Line** tab, remove the outline from the shape by clicking ⊞ **None** from the line style drop-down list.

10 On the Drawing toolbar, click ☆ **Filter Effects**.

11 In the **Filter Effects** dialog:

- In the **Effects** list, select **Bevel and Emboss**.

- In the **Style** box, select **Inner Bevel**.

- For the **Highlight**, select Normal, white, and 80% opacity.

- For the **Shadow,** select Normal, white, and 80% opacity.

- Set the **Blur** to 15, the **Depth** to 200, **Soften** to 0, **Angle** to 90, and **Elevation** to 45.

- Click **OK**.

12 Click the  **Pointer** tool, select the lozenge, then type some text inside the shape (this is **shape text**).

13 Format your text as desired. (You can't change the outline colour of shape text, so if you want to do this, you'll need to use the **A Artistic Text** tool to create **artistic text**.)

14 Right-click your newly created button and click **Insert Slice Object**. 'Slice lines' now display on your page, defining the button as a separate web object.

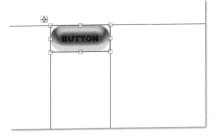

15 Double-click the shaded interior region of your button to open the **Image Slice Object Properties** dialog.

16 In the **Rollover Details** section, click to select the **Over** and **Down** check boxes and click **OK**.

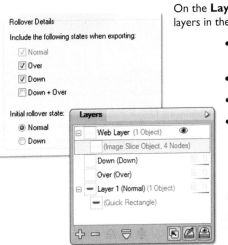

On the **Layers** tab, you'll now see four layers in the document:

- **Web Layer**—containing the image slice object

- **Down**

- **Over**

- **Normal**—containing the Quick Rectangle

> For future reference, note that slice objects can be moved, resized, and edited just like normal objects.

The Image Slice Properties dialog

Use this dialog, to define the various states and actions that will be associated with a button when it's on a web page. The **URL** box usually defines a hyperlink target page, and the **Text** box stores a popup 'tooltip' message displayed on a rollover event. In the **Rollover Details** section you can select how many button states you want to be active.

- **Normal**—this is the standard state of the graphic before any rollover, and is always included.

- **Over**—the state triggered by a mouseover.

- **Down**—the state triggered by a mouse click on the graphic.

Down + Over is rarely used.

We already have a graphic on our **Normal** layer, so all we need to do now is create a variant state (a different graphic) on the **Over** and **Down** layers—for the rollover states we intend to activate.

17 Select the button object, copy it from the **Normal** layer, then on the **Layers** tab, click the **Over** layer to switch to that layer.

18 Paste the copy on to the **Over** layer (the button will appear in precise alignment with the original). On the **Swatch** tab, apply a different fill colour.

19 Click the **Down** layer tab, paste again, and apply another colour.

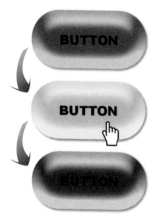

At this point you can preview your efforts in a web browser.

20 On the **File** menu, click **Preview in Browser**. This launches your default browser and displays the button onscreen.

21 Roll your mouse over the button and click to see the variant 'Over' and 'Down' graphics you defined.

To export the button along with its defined rollover states

1   On the **Normal** layer, select the slice object and on the **File** menu, click **Export > Export as Image**.

2   In the **Export Optimizer** dialog, in the **Format** drop-down list, select an appropriate file type (typically JPG, GIF, JPEG, or PNG) and choose your settings.

3   On the **Settings** tab:

   • Use a **dpi** of 96 (customary for onscreen graphics).

   • Select the **Image Slices** check box.

   • Click **Export**.

Congratulations, you've exported your web button along with its rollover states!

DrawPlus creates a file for each image state, and a single file containing the HTML code, from which you can copy and paste <head> and <body> sections into the corresponding sections of your web page.

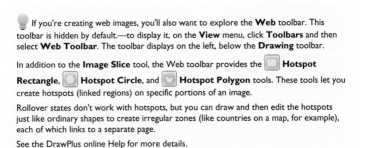

💡 If you're creating web images, you'll also want to explore the **Web** toolbar. This toolbar is hidden by default.—to display it, on the **View** menu, click **Toolbars** and then select **Web Toolbar**. The toolbar displays on the left, below the **Drawing** toolbar.

In addition to the **Image Slice** tool, the Web toolbar provides the 🖼 **Hotspot Rectangle,** 🔘 **Hotspot Circle**, and ⬡ **Hotspot Polygon** tools. These tools let you create hotspots (linked regions) on specific portions of an image.

Rollover states don't work with hotspots, but you can draw and then edit the hotspots just like ordinary shapes to create irregular zones (like countries on a map, for example), each of which links to a separate page.

See the DrawPlus online Help for more details.

Creating a
Keyframe Animation

DrawPlus X3 provides exciting functionality that lets you create and export Adobe® Flash®-based animations using keyframes. Combine this with the extensive drawing capabilities of DrawPlus, and you have all the tools you need to create impressive movies, cartoons, Web banners, and so on.

This exercise introduces you to the basic concepts and essential tools, and shows you how to create a simple animated cartoon. You'll learn how to:

- Create a cartoon character using the DrawPlus drawing tools.
- Work with layers and grouping.
- Use keyframes to animate a character.
- Use the AutoRun feature to automatically update object creation and placement as you work.
- Use an object envelope to modify an object's rate of change over time.
- Add a background.
- Export to Adobe® Shockwave Flash® format.

💡 You can view the sample DrawPlus file we created for this project (**Dog_animation.dpa**) and the output file (**Dog_animation.swf**) in the ...**Workspace\Animation** folder of your DrawPlus installation.

In a default installation, you'll find this folder in the following location:

C:\Program Files\Serif\DrawPlus\X3\Tutorials

You can also use DrawPlus to produce stopframe animations. See the *Creating a Stopframe Animation* tutorial, available from the Tutorials contents screen. (To open the contents screen, click **Help > Tutorials**.)

Introduction

The term **stopframe** (or **stop motion**) animation describes the conventional animation technique that makes static objects appear to move. The object is moved by very small amounts in successive frames, giving the impression of movement when the film is played.

In **keyframe** animation, a particular event or sequence of events is recreated in a series of snapshot images. The event is 'captured' at key moments (keyframes) where an object begins or ends an action. Animation between these keyframes is then calculated by the software—in this case, DrawPlus.

For example, suppose you want to create an animation of a bouncing ball. As the animator, you specify the start, end, and key intermediary positions of the ball, then DrawPlus smoothly fills in the gaps (a process known as **tweening**). At any point, you can fine-tune the animation to improve the duration, speed, and dynamics of the movement by adding or adjusting keyframes.

In the following sections, we'll use the same technique to animate a simple character. Before we can get started on the animation phase of our project, however, there are a few things we need to do.

1: Storyboarding

A storyboard is a visual script of the shots and scene changes in a video or film—a plan that you can refer to as you work on your project.

The storyboarding process helps you to think about how you want your finished animation to look, how the story should unfold, and how best to convey your story to your audience.

Think about what you actually want to achieve, and then create a rough illustration of what will happen during the animation. You don't have to be an artist—rough sketches and stick figures will do just as well.

The storyboard on the left illustrates the animation we are about to create.

2: Starting the project and drawing the character

To begin, let's open DrawPlus, start a new animation project and then draw our character.

To start a new keyframe animation

1   On the **File** menu, point to **New**, then click **New Keyframe Animation**.

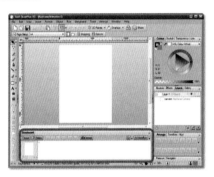

DrawPlus creates the first keyframe for the project and displays it in the main work area and on the **Storyboard** tab at the lower edge of the workspace.

(If you can't see the **Storyboard** tab, click the **Open/Close** button at the bottom of the workspace.)

2   On the context toolbar, click ☐ **Landscape** page orientation. Now to create our character.

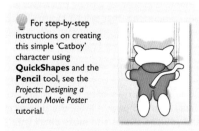

💡 For step-by-step instructions on creating this simple 'Catboy' character using **QuickShapes** and the **Pencil** tool, see the *Projects: Designing a Cartoon Movie Poster* tutorial.

This stage is quite personal. Some designers prefer to sketch their rough ideas with pencil and paper first, while others prefer to work directly with the DrawPlus drawing tools. We suggest you experiment with both techniques to see which you prefer. (Initially, we'll just concentrate on creating and animating the dog character. We'll discuss backgrounds later in the tutorial.)

- If you're sketching with DrawPlus tools, we recommend you use **QuickShapes** for drawing simple shapes, the 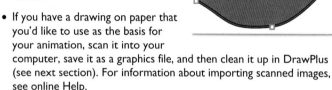 **Pencil** tool for drawing freeform lines and shapes, and the **Pen** tool for precise lines.

- You can fine-tune any line or curve by switching to the **Node** tool and then adjusting the nodes and curves.

- If you have a drawing on paper that you'd like to use as the basis for your animation, scan it into your computer, save it as a graphics file, and then clean it up in DrawPlus (see next section). For information about importing scanned images, see online Help.

- If you're using a pen and tablet but are not too sure of your freehand drawing ability, you can place a printed image on the tablet and trace around its outlines, or draw accurate lines by using a ruler on the tablet.

- If you want to use the character used in this project, you'll find the sample file (**Dog_original.png**) in your ...\Animation folder.

3: Cleaning up your sketch

When you have created your rough sketch, the next task is to clean up the outlines and shapes. During this stage, you also want to identify and isolate the components that will be moving independently—if you do this, you'll find it easier to adjust and manipulate these parts as you work on your animation keyframes later.

These components will vary depending on your character and story, and will range from the obvious—for example, body, legs, head—to the not so obvious (eyebrows, ears, hair, lips, and so on). Don't go into too much detail at first though. Often, the simpler characters are the most effective, and you can always add more detail later if necessary.

The following tips will help you to achieve the best results:

- If you're working from a scanned image, place your original sketch on Layer 1, add a new layer and then work on this layer as you carefully trace over the original lines.

  When you've finished, hide the layer containing the original sketch to check your results.

- Use **QuickShapes** for simple shapes.

  If necessary, use the **Convert to Curves** command on the **Arrange** tab, and then use the **Node** tool to adjust the shape. You can do this by clicking and dragging the nodes, curve segments, and control handles. The following illustration shows how we created the basic ear shape from a simple **Quick Ellipse**.

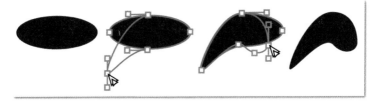

- When using the **Pencil** tool, increase the **Smoothness** on the context toolbar. This reduces the number of nodes on the line, resulting in a 'cleaner,' smoother effect. (We set **Smoothness** to 100%.)

⭐ **Optimizing file size**

- To keep your Flash files as small as possible, you should avoid using special effects such as filter effects, shadows, 3D, transparency, bitmap fills, and so on, which are also output as bitmaps.

- You can achieve some great simple 'hand-drawn effect' animations with the **Paintbrush** tool. However, you should try to avoid using the **Paintbrush** if you intend exporting your project to Flash format. This is because brushstrokes are output as bitmaps and will result in a large file size.

- **Group** your items.

  When you've finished drawing the various lines and shapes that make up each component, select them all, then click the Group button below the selection.

  You'll now be able to move and rotate all the objects in the group at the same time. You'll find this useful when you are animating the project.

(To select and edit individual objects within groups, hold down the **Ctrl** key and then click to select.)

- If you need to rotate a component or group of components that are 'hinged' from a fixed point—a leg, arm, or head for example—you'll achieve a more realistic effect if you move the centre of rotation to the hinge point.

  To do this, select the object or group and then click and drag the **rotation origin** to the desired position. You can then rotate the object from a corner selection handle.

  The illustration below shows how we could use this technique to rotate the head of our cartoon dog.

When drawing your character, the following tips will help you achieve the best results:

- Keep it simple and use clean lines and shapes. You can create a detailed version first, to get a good feel for your character, but before you start animating it, you'll need to simplify it. The simpler your character is, the easier it will be to animate.

- Keep your colours simple and in blocks rather than random lines. This will make it easier for you to blend the moving elements of your drawing, and will also help minimize your final file size.

- Use shadows to 'ground' and add depth to your animation. Without shadows, your characters will appear to float.

- If your character is going to talk, you'll need to draw variations of the mouth for different 'sounds.' If you don't require too much detail, you can get by with a few basic mouth shapes—A, E, I, O, U, F, M, P, S, TH, and so on. You'll also need some transition shapes to take you from one mouth form to the next.

You may need to move small body parts individually at times, but you'll save yourself a lot of effort by creating groups of parts that you can move and rotate together.

These illustrations show our initial sketch and the finished character after tracing and redrawing.

Notice how the addition of the shadow grounds the character and adds depth to the animation.

4: Animating the character

When you are happy with your character, you're ready to animate it.

1 On the **Storyboard** tab, click [⏺ Insert].

2 In the **Insert Keyframes** dialog:

- In the **Number of keyframes** box, enter **6**.

- In the **Keyframe duration** box, enter **0.333**.

- Click **OK**.

You'll now see seven keyframes on the **Storyboard** tab.

Let's refer to our storyboard to see which parts of the dog we need to adjust. In our example, the head and face have not changed, only the legs have moved.

3 In **keyframe 1**, select all of the objects that make up the dog and his shadow. Click **Edit** and then click **Copy** (or click **Ctrl + C**).

4 Click **keyframe 2** to open in the work area. On the **Layers** tab, click ➕ **Add Layer**.

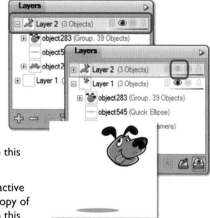

- Make **Layer 2** the active layer by clicking it on the **Layers** tab to highlight it. Click **Edit** and then click **Paste** (or click **Ctrl + V**) to copy the dog and shadow onto this layer.

- Now make **Layer 1** the active layer and paste another copy of the dog and shadow onto this layer. Delete the body and legs.

To check that you've done this correctly, hide Layer 2 by clicking its ◉ **Hide/Show** button—you will only see the dog's head and shadow.

5 On Layer 1, draw the 'new' body and legs shape. Use the body shape on Layer 2 as a reference to ensure that the parts of the body that do not move (the upper chest and back for example), remain in the same position on the page.

Check your progress by periodically hiding the original drawing on Layer 2.

When you have completed your drawing on Layer 1, you can delete Layer 2 by selecting it on the **Layers** tab and then clicking ➖ **Delete Layer**.

6 Copy and paste the dog and shadow from keyframe **1** onto keyframes **3**, **5** and **7**.

7 Copy and paste the dog and shadow from keyframe **2** onto keyframes **4** and **6**.

You're storyboard should now resemble ours.

8 Open keyframe **6** in the work area. In this scene, the dog is hit by the bone.

You can keep the basic head shape, but need to redraw the eyes and ears and add the 'bash' star shape.

When you've completed all the changes you need to make to the dog, you can add the bone...

9 On the **Storyboard** tab, click the ▷▷ AutoRun ▼ button to enable this feature.

By default, any new objects you create (and reposition) on any keyframe will now automatically run to the end of the storyboard.

10 Open keyframe 2 in the work area and draw and colour the bone.

Place it in the upper left corner so that only the end is visible.

If you now take a look at your storyboard, you'll see that DrawPlus has placed a copy of the bone in all subsequent keyframes.

11 Open keyframe 3. Click on the bone to select it, and then drag it slightly down and to the right.

Hover your cursor just outside one of the corner handles. When the cursor changes to the Rotate cursor, click and drag to rotate the bone.

Because you have **AutoRun** enabled, DrawPlus updates the placement of the bone in subsequent keyframes, allowing you to easily make incremental changes to its position.

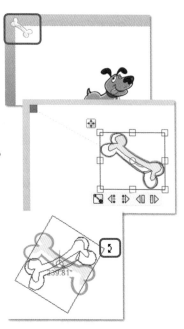

12 Repeat step 14 to move and rotate the bone through the remaining frames. Remember that it should hit the dog's head in keyframe 6, and then bounce off in keyframe 7.

Notice the path and nodes showing the movement of the bone through the scene.

13 To preview your animation, on the **Storyboard** tab, in the Preview drop-down list, click **Preview in Flash Player**.

14 If required, make any adjustments to the placement of the bone. Preview your animation until you are happy with the results and then click the ⟦ᗞᗞ AutoRun ▼⟧ button to turn this feature off again.

When you preview your animation, you'll see that the dog and bone both move at a constant speed throughout the entire animation. This may be the effect you require, but suppose you want to vary the speed of an object as it moves through a scene. In the next section, we'll show you how to do this.

5: Adjusting object envelopes

When you select an object that is part of a 'run sequence' (such as the bone in our animation), the **Easing** tab becomes available.

In DrawPlus keyframe animations, the **Easing** tab provides a drop-down list of **envelopes** (Position, Morph, Scale, Rotation, Skew, Colour, and Transparency).

All of these envelopes work in similar ways to control how an object's properties change over time, from keyframe to keyframe. Once you learn how to display and modify one type of envelope, you can apply the same principle to the others.

By default, DrawPlus applies a constant rate of change to all envelopes, but you can adjust this by modifying the envelope profile settings.

The lower section of the **Easing** tab provides various other options that you can apply to the selected object or to the whole run.

In this section, we'll make the bone object appear to accelerate as it bounces off the dog's head by applying and modifying a **position envelope**.

To apply a position envelope

1 Open keyframe 6 and select the bone object.

2 On the **Easing** tab, expand the Envelopes drop-down list and select the **Position Envelope**. (If you can't see the **Easing** tab, you may need to expand it by clicking ┃ next to the Drawing toolbar.)

Below the drop-down list, in the Envelope Profile pane, the blue diagonal line represents the rate of change of the bone's position from this keyframe to the next.

By default, the rate of change is constant, but we can change this by adjusting the gradient of the profile.

3   Click a point in the middle of the blue line and drag it up to the top of the pane. (You may find it easier to undock and then expand the **Easing** tab to adjust the profile.)

4   Preview your animation again.

You should see the bone speed up as it bounces off the dog's head.

6: Adding a background

You may not need or want a background for your animation. It all depends on your subject matter and the final effect you want to achieve.

A background will provide 'context' for your character, but can also be useful for adding perspective and depth to a scene. There are several ways to do this, for example:

• Use strong (saturated) colours for your character and foreground, and less strong (unsaturated) colours for background objects. (See our circular background below.)

• Make foreground elements sharp and clear and your background elements blurred.

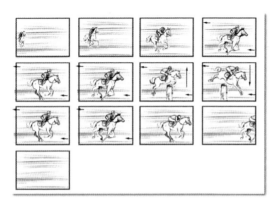

Backgrounds don't have to be detailed. In this racehorse storyboard, the roughly-sketched background gives the impression of motion and speed.

In some cases, a background will reduce the impact of the scene.

Suppose you are animating a stick figure such as the one pictured. Here, you want the viewer's attention to be focused on the character and nothing else.

If you do use a background, place it on a separate layer, underneath all of your other layers.

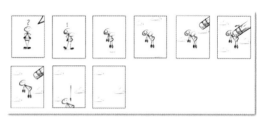

We created a colourful circular background, which rotated throughout the run sequence.

To add and rotate a circular background

1   Create your background as a DrawPlus .dpp file and export it to .png file format.

2   In your animation, add a new layer and move it down to the bottom of the layers list.

3   On the background layer, click ▣ **Insert Picture** and position your background graphic.

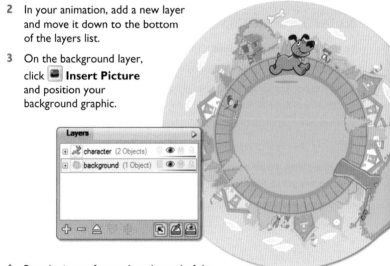

4   Run the image forward to the end of the storyboard by clicking ▷▷ **Run Forward**.

5 Open the last keyframe, select the background graphic, and then rotate it into its final position. DrawPlus will calculate the steps in between for you.

As it stands, this is a short seven-frame animation, so you don't need to make the rotation angle too big. (If you do want to rotate through the full 360°, you'll need to insert more keyframes—we needed 17 for our example—so that the speed of the rotation is appropriate for the speed of the running dog.)

6 Preview your animation and make any adjustments to the rotation angle if required.

If you're looking for something simpler, you could add a linear background scene.

To add a linear background

1 Repeat steps 1 to 4 of the previous procedure.

2 In the last keyframe, select the background graphic and drag it to the left and into its final position.

3 Preview your animation and make any adjustments if required.

If you're happy with your animation, you're ready to export it.

7: Exporting your animation
You can export to the following formats:

- Adobe Shockwave Flash file (.swf)
- Video (choose from .mov, .stv, .avi, .wmf file formats)
- Screensaver (.scr)
- Flash Lite/ i-Mode (a lightweight version of .swf, optimized for viewing on mobile phones and other devices)
- Image (a wide range of formats are supported, see online Help for details)

As well as showing changes in position and rotation, you can use keyframes to show changes in colour.

Simply set the start and end colours in separate keyframes and DrawPlus will use tweening to calculate the blend from one colour to the next. You may also want to add an extra keyframe or two for transition stages, as we've done in this example.

To change the rate at which an object's colour changes over time, adjust its colour envelope. For example, you could make the blush on this character's face appear quickly and fade away slowly.

For this project, we will export our animation to a standard Shockwave Flash .swf file.

To export to Adobe Shockwave Flash

1   On the **File** menu, point to **Export** and then click **Export as Flash SWF**.

2   Choose a file name and save location for your .swf file and then click **Save**.

3   The **Keyframe Animation Export** dialog displays the progress of the export and closes when export is complete. .

    Simply browse to locate the file and then double-click to open it.

We hope that you have enjoyed working through this project and are happy with the resulting animation. We hope that you are now comfortable with the basics of keyframe animation and are ready to begin experimenting with your own projects.

If you'd like to work through some more step-by-step examples, take a look at the other tutorials in the **Animation & Web** section.

Creating a Movie Viewer

Use keyframe animation to create a movie viewer that you can add to your website and use to view a movie clip of your choice.

You'll learn how to:

- Create, edit, and align shapes.
- Use state objects to create **Play** and **Stop** buttons.
- Import movie clips.
- Add action scripts.
- Export your file to Adobe® Flash® file format.

You can use your own movie clip for this project, or our sample, which you'll find in the **Workspace\Animation** folder of your DrawPlus installation directory. In a standard installation, you'll find this folder in the following location:

C:\Program Files\Serif\DrawPlus\X3\Tutorials\Workspace\Animation

Introduction

By default, any object created in DrawPlus is considered to be a **non-state object**, possessing a single set of attributes—colour, transparency, and so on. In keyframe animation, however, you can convert a non-state object to a **state object** by assigning it one or more 'states' (**Normal**, **Hover**, or **Pressed**), each of which possessing its own object attributes.

The key advantage here is that in each state, the object can have a different appearance in response to a user event such as a mouse press or mouse hover over.

In DrawPlus, an object's state is indicated by its adjacent state buttons (only two states will be shown at any time; the third state is the current state).

For example, an object in **Normal** state shows adjacent **Hover** and **Pressed** buttons. If you then click the **Hover** button, you'll jump to that state and the **Normal** and **Pressed** state buttons will display.

In this simple exercise, we'll show you how to create a movie viewer and use state objects to create **Play** and **Stop** buttons that allow you to play and stop a movie clip inside the viewer.

You can insert a movie clip into any animation. The movie is inserted into your chosen keyframe as an object, which you can run forward through a specified number of keyframes, or through the entire storyboard, as required.

DrawPlus supports various video formats including .flv, .avi, .mov, .wmv, .mpg, and .swf.

To create the viewer

1   On the **File** menu, point to **New** and then click **New Keyframe Animation**.

2   On the Page context toolbar, click ⚹ Page Setup .

3   In the **Keyframe Animation Page Setup** dialog, in the **Dimensions** section, set the Width and Height to 350 pix. Click **OK**.

4   On the Drawing toolbar, on the QuickShape flyout, click the
    ☐▾ **Quick Rectangle**. Draw a
    rectangle 335 pix x 280 pix.

5   With the shape selected:

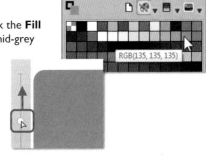

•   On the **Swatch** tab, click the **Fill**
    button and then click a mid-grey
    swatch to apply it to the
    shape (we used **RGB
    135, 135, 135**).

•   On the **Line** tab click
    ⊞ **None**.

•   On the shape, drag the
    node up to round the
    corners.

6   Right-click the shape and then click **Copy**. Right-click again and click
    Paste.

    DrawPlus pastes a copy of your shape directly on top of the original
    and selects it by default.

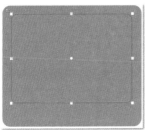

7   Working with the copied shape, click
    and drag a corner handle to resize it
    to 290 pix x 205 pix.

8   Position the smaller shape so that
    there is equal space at the top and
    sides of the shape—we'll add
    controls to the larger area at the
    bottom. Click **Edit**, then **Select All**
    to select both objects, then do the
    following:

•   On the **Align** tab click
    🔲 **Centre Horizontally**.

•   On the **Arrange** tab, click
    🔲 **Subtract**.

The inner rectangle is used like a "cookie
cutter" to leave a hole in the shape.

9 With the new shape selected, on the **Effects** tab, select the **Plastic** category and click **Plastic 8**.

10 Position the viewer towards the bottom of the page as illustrated.

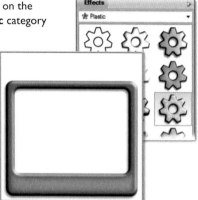

This creates the basic TV shape for the viewer. Let's give it an aerial...

To create the aerial

1 On the Drawing toolbar, click **Quick Ellipse**.

2 To create the aerial base:

- Draw a small ellipse approximately 65 pix wide and 20 pix high. If necessary, apply the same mid-grey fill that you used before.

- Position the shape so that half of it is over the viewer and half of it is above.

- On the **Effects** tab, click to apply the same **Plastic 8** effect.

3 To create the antennae:

- On the Drawing toolbar, click the **Straight Line** tool and on the **Swatch** tab, set the line colour to black.

- Draw two lines coming out of the ellipse in a "V" shape.

- Click to select the **Pointer** tool and then, select the lines and on the **Arrange** tab, click **Send to Back**.

4 To create the ends:

- On the Drawing toolbar, click **Quick Ellipse** and at the top of the first line draw a 12 pix x 12 pix circle.

- On the **Swatch** tab, change the fill to bright yellow.

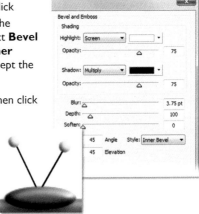

- On the Drawing toolbar, click **Filter Effects** and in the **Filter Effects** dialog, select **Bevel and Emboss**. Choose **Inner Bevel** and click **OK** to accept the default settings.

- Right-click the shape and then click **Copy**. Right-click again and click **Paste**. As before, a copy of your shape is places directly on top of the original. Drag this new shape into position at the top of the second line.

5 Your aerial is almost complete. Drag a selection box around all of the components of the aerial and click Group.

6 Your aerial should have been positioned at the back of the viewer. If not, on the **Arrange** tab, click **Send to Back**.

Now we have created our TV viewer, let's add a movie...

To insert the movie

1   On the Drawing toolbar, click  **Insert Movie Clip**.

2   In the **Insert Movie Clip** dialog:

- Navigate to your ...**\Animation** folder (or to the folder containing your own movie file).

- In the **Files of type** drop-down list, select **SWF movie (*.swf)** (or the file type for the movie clip you want to insert).

- Select **dog.swf** (or your own file) and click **Open**.

3   On your page, position the displayed cursor in the upper left corner of your movie viewer, then click to insert the movie at its original size.

   (Click and drag out to set the size of the movie inside the viewer, while maintaining its aspect ratio.)

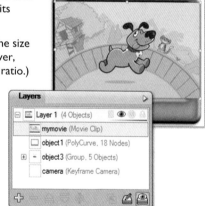

4   On the **Layers** tab, locate your movie clip object and then click on its name to highlight it. Rename the clip 'mymovie.'

5   With the clip still selected, on the **Arrange** tab, click **Send to Back**. Fine tune the movie size if needed.

6   On the Storyboard tab, in the ▷▾ **Preview** drop-down list, select **Preview in Flash Player**.

   You should see your movie playing.

To quickly replace your movie clip:

1 On the **Media** tab, in the drop-down list, choose **Movie Clips**. The lower section of the tab displays your clip.

2 Right click on the clip and choose **Replace Media**. Browse to locate the replacement file and click **Open**.

To create the state object buttons

1 On the Drawing toolbar, click the ⃝ **Quick Ellipse** and draw a small circle in the lower right area of the viewer.

- On the **Swatch** tab, set the Line and Fill colour to red.

- On the Drawing toolbar, click ⭐ **Filter Effects** and in the **Filter Effects** dialog, select **Bevel and Emboss**.

  In the **Style** drop-down list, choose **Pillow Emboss** and then click **OK** to accept the default settings.

2 Right-click the circle and then click **Copy**. Right-click again and click **Paste**. Drag the copy into position next to the original.

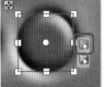

- On the **Swatch** tab, set the Line and Fill colour to green.

3 Move and size the shapes so that they resemble Stop and Play buttons. Select both objects and then on the **Align** tab, click ⬚ **Centre Vertically**.

4 Select the red circle. On the **Object** menu, choose **State** and then click **Convert to state object**.

5 On the state object toolbar, click the ⬚ **Hover** state button. Now let's set the attributes for this button when the user hovers the mouse over it.

6 On the Drawing toolbar, click  **Filter Effects**. In the **Filter Effects** dialog:

- Select the **Outer Glow** check box.

- Set the **Blur** to 12 and the **Intensity** to 5.

- Set the colour to red.

- Select the **Colour Fill** check box.

- Set the **Blend Mode** to **Screen**.

- Set the colour to red.

- Click **OK**.

7 Select the green circle. Repeat steps 4 to 6, this time setting the outer glow and colour fill colour to green.

8 Select the red circle. On the **Actions** tab, double-click **Mouse Press**.

9 In the **Mouse Press** dialog, in the left **Available Actions** pane:

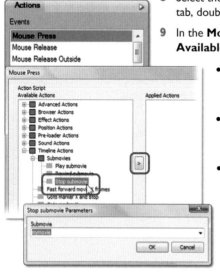

- Expand the **Timeline Actions**, then **Submovies** categories.

- Double-click the **Stop Movie** action (or press the **Add** button).

- In the **Stop submovie Parameters** dialog, select **mymovie** from the drop-down list and click **OK**.

💡 In the default profile, the **Actions** tab is found on the left of the studio workspace. If you can't see it, you may need to expand the studio tab by clicking ▌. You can also choose one of the Keyframe animation Workspace profiles from the **View** menu. Go to **View>Studio Tabs>Load Workspace...**

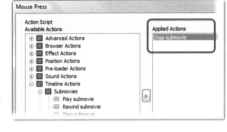

The **Stop Movie** action is added to the **Applied Actions** pane on the right.

- Click **OK** to close the **Mouse Press (Object)** dialog.

10 Select the green circle. Repeat steps 8 and 9, this time selecting the **Play submovie** action.

11 Preview your animation.

Your movie should stop and play when you click the appropriate button. Hovering over the buttons will show the glow effect.

We'll finish the tutorial by exporting the movie to a Flash SWF file.

To export as Flash

1   On the **File** menu, point to **Export** and then click **Export as Flash SWF...**

2   Choose a file name and save location for your *.swf file and then click **Save**.

3   The **Keyframe Animation Export** dialog displays the progress of the export and closes when export is complete.

4   Browse to locate the exported *.swf file.

5   If your computer has an application associated with *.swf files, you can simply double-click the file to open it.

    - or -

    Right-click the file, click **Open With...** and then choose your web browser application from the list of installed programs.

That's it! We hope you enjoyed creating your movie viewer and that it's given you some ideas to experiment with on your own. If you haven't done so already, take a look at some of the other tutorials in the **Animation & Web** section.

Creating an Animated Web Banner

You don't have to be an experienced DrawPlus user to create impressive animation effects.

In this project, we'll show you how to use masks and transparency effects to create professional-looking results. We'll create a Web banner similar to one of our templates, but you can apply the same techniques to any animation project.

By the end of the tutorial, you'll be able to:

- Apply and customize a gradient fill.
- Create and format text.
- Add transparency effects.
- Use a mask to gradually reveal an object on the page.
- Fit text to a curve.
- Work with layers and grouping.
- Preview and export to Adobe® Flash® format.

You can view the sample file we created for this project
(**Arts_&_Crafts_animation.dpa**) in the **...\Workspace\Animation** folder of your DrawPlus installation.

In a default installation, you'll find this folder in the following location:

C:\Program Files\Serif\DrawPlus\X3\Tutorials

We created our Web banner on five layers. To make it easier to follow, this tutorial is divided into sections, each of which will explain how to create a different layer.

Layer 1: Background

On this layer, we'll create the background elements of our design—the gradient filled rectangle with its brush stroke effect outline, and the large green letter R.

1   On the **File** menu, point to **New** and then click **New Keyframe Animation**.

2   On the Page context toolbar, set the following page options:

   • In the Page Size drop-down list, click **Full Banner**.

   • Click the ▭ **Landscape** button.

3   On the Drawing toolbar, on the QuickShape flyout, click the
     ▭▾ **Quick Rectangle** and draw a large rectangle that fills the page.

4   With the rectangle selected, click the **Swatch** tab. In the
     ▪▾ **Gradient** drop-down list, click **Radial**, and then click the **Radial 1** swatch.

5   On the Drawing toolbar, click the ◈ **Fill** tool to display the fill path and nodes.

     Drag the right node to the left and into position just below the page border. Drag the left node to the right.

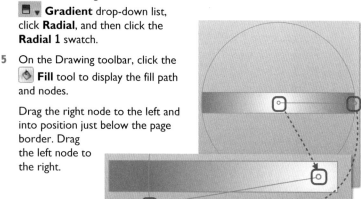

6 On the **Swatch** tab, click the ▷ **Swatch Tab Menu** and select **List View**. In the 🎨 ▾ **Palettes** drop-down list, click **Standard RGB**. Scroll down the palette to locate the **RGB (156, 156, 0)** swatch and then click and drag it over to the leftmost node of your fill path.

Now find the **RGB (252, 252, 156)** swatch and click and drag it over to the rightmost node of your fill path.

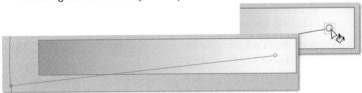

7 On the Drawing toolbar, click the **A** **Artistic Text** tool.

Click and drag on your page to create a large text insertion point, then type the first letter of your banner logo in uppercase.

8 Triple-click the text to select it, then format as follows:

• On the Text context toolbar, change the font to something fairly ornate.

• On the **Swatch** tab, apply the **RGB (156, 156, 0)** swatch.

• If required, resize the text by clicking and dragging a corner handle.

9 Click the 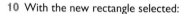 **Quick Rectangle** and draw another rectangle the same size as your first shape.

10 With the new rectangle selected:

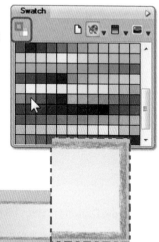

- On the **Swatch** tab, remove the fill by clicking the grey and white **None** swatch.

- On the **Swatch** tab, click the **Line** swatch and then click the **RGB (132, 132, 0)** swatch.

- On the **Brushes** tab, click the **Charcoal 05 brush** stroke to apply it to the outline.

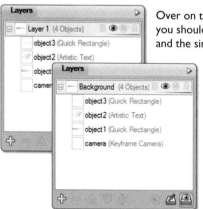

Over on the **Layers** tab, under **Layer 1**, you should now see the two rectangles and the single text object listed.

11 On the **Layers** tab, right-click the **Mask** layer and click **Layer Properties**. Rename your layer 'Background.' Click **OK**.

Let's move on and create our next layer.

You'll also see the **Keyframe Camera** object on Layer 1. You can use this to create some great pan and zoom effects. We won't be using it in this project, but for a quick and simple example, see the **How To** tab.

Layer 2: Swish

On our second layer, we'll add the ornate curved 'swish' design.

1   On the **Layers** tab, click ⊞ **Add Layer**.

    Rename the new layer 'Swish.'

2   On the Drawing toolbar, click the 🖊 **Pen** tool and then click to
    create a large closed curved shape across your page. Fill the shape with
    RGB (156, 156, 0).

    Don't worry about drawing a perfect shape—you can edit it in the
    next step.

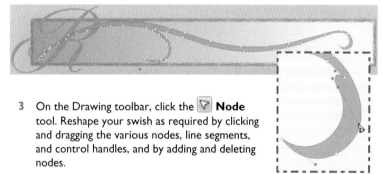

3   On the Drawing toolbar, click the ▽ **Node**
    tool. Reshape your swish as required by clicking
    and dragging the various nodes, line segments,
    and control handles, and by adding and deleting
    nodes.

4   To complete this layer,
    use the 🖊 **Pen** tool to
    create some leaf shapes,
    and add a white
    ◯ **Quick Ellipse**.

🔖 The **Pen** tool is a powerful tool that you can use in several different ways. Once
you've drawn your curve or shape, you can fine-tune it with the **Node** tool—again, using
several different methods.

For details, see the **How To** tab or online Help. For a step-by-step exercise, see the
Mastering the Basics: Working with Line Tools tutorial.

Layer 3: Mask

We'll create our mask on layer three, using it to gradually display the elements we've created on our **Swish** layer.

1   On the **Layers** tab, click ✚ **Add Layer**. Rename the new layer 'Mask.'

2   Working on the **Mask** layer, click the ▢▾ **Quick Rectangle** and draw a long, narrow rectangle to cover the start of the swish.

This rectangle shape will act as a 'window' through which the swish will appear.

3   With the mask shape selected, on the **Swatch** tab, apply a bright colour to the fill and outline.

It doesn't matter what colour you choose for your mask as it won't be seen in the final animation. However, when working with masks, it's generally a good idea to make them bright and easily identifiable (especially when working on complex projects).

4   At the bottom of the workspace, on the **Storyboard** tab, click ⊙ Insert .

In the **Insert Keyframes** dialog, choose to insert 1 keyframe with a duration of 3.5 seconds and click **OK**.

On the **Storyboard** tab, DrawPlus adds a new keyframe containing all of your design elements, and displays the project length as 3500 milliseconds (3.5 seconds).

5   With the first keyframe still selected, on the **Storyboard** tab, click ▯▯ **Split**. In the **Split Keyframe** dialog, type '6' and click **OK**.

All your design elements, including the mask, now run right through to the end of the animation.

6 On the **Storyboard** tab, click on the last keyframe to open it in the workspace. On the **Layers** tab, click on the **Mask** layer.

7 Select the mask object, then click and drag the right sizing handle until the shape completely covers the swish.

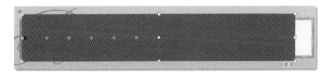

8 On the **Layers** tab, right-click the **Mask** layer and click **Layer Properties**. In the **Layer Properties** dialog, in the **Attributes** section:

- Select the **Locked** check box.

- Select the **Mask** check box and then in the drop-down layers list, select **1**.

  This tells DrawPlus that we want this layer to only mask one layer beneath it. (If we'd chosen to mask 2 layers, the mask would also hide objects on the **Background** layer.)

- Click **OK**.

On the **Layers** tab, the 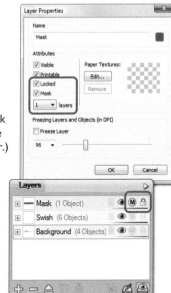 Mask and Locked icons now display next to the **Mask** layer. The colour of the layers also change to clearly show the mask layer and the layer being masked.

9 On the **Storyboard** tab, in the Preview list, click **Preview in Flash Player**.

10 If necessary, in the first and last keyframes, adjust the start and end position and size of the mask until you're happy with the way in which it reveals the swish.

Now we'll add two more layers **above** our mask layer.

Layer 4: Logo

On our next layer, we'll add our logo and some flower shapes. We don't want these elements to appear immediately, so we'll stagger their appearance on the storyboard.

1 On the **Layers** tab:

- Click  **Add Layer**. Rename the new layer 'Logo & Flowers.'

- Next to the **Mask** layer, click the 🔒 **Lock** button. This will unlock (deactivate) the mask and your mask shape will be revealed. Click the 👁 **Hide/Show** layer button to hide the mask completely so that you can see the entire swish on all your keyframes. (You don't have to do this but it helps to see the whole design while you are adding new elements to it—it won't affect the export or preview.)

2 Open keyframe 4 in the workspace.

- Click the **A Artistic Text** tool and create a logo in the left section of the banner, on top of your background letter.

  - Apply the same font as before and resize the logo text to 32 pt.

- On the **Swatch** tab, in the ▦ **Gradient** drop-down list, click **Linear** and then apply the **Linear 119** swatch.

- On the **Colour** tab, set the **Opacity slider** to 80%.

3 Click the 🖊 **Pen** tool.

Use your preferred drawing method to create a flower head out of a series of closed and filled curves.

4 Select all the elements that make up your flower head and then click the Group 🔲 button.

5 With the flower selected, on the **Colour** tab, set the **Opacity slider** to 70%.

6 Copy and paste the flower head and set the **Opacity slider** to 25%.

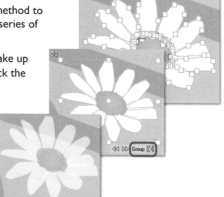

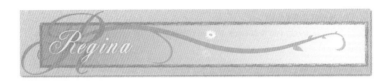

7   Position the two flower heads in the middle section of the banner.

8   On the **Edit** menu, click **Select All** to select the logo and both flowers.

   - To the lower right of the selection, click ▷▷ **Run Forward**. In the **Run Forward** dialog, select **To end of storyboard** and click **OK**.

   - On the **Storyboard** tab, if you now click through the keyframes, you'll see that DrawPlus has run these three objects right through to the last keyframe.

9   Right-click one of the flower heads and click **Copy**.

   - Open keyframe 3 in the workplace, then right-click on the page and click **Paste** to add a copy of the flower to this keyframe.

   - Increase the size of the copied flower.

   - On the **Colour** tab, set the **Opacity slider** to **78%**.

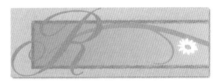

   - Position the flower as illustrated, right.

   - Select the flower, then click ▷▷ **Run Forward**. In the **Run Forward** dialog, select **To end of storyboard** and click **OK**.

10 Open keyframe 5 and add another copy of the flower.

   - Position the flower towards the end of the swish shape.

   - Select the flower, then click ▷▷ **Run Forward** and in the **Run Forward** dialog, select **To end of storyboard**. Click **OK**.

11 Preview your animation and make any adjustments, as required.

Just one more layer to create...

5: Text on a curve

On our final layer, we'll create a text object and fit it to the curve of the swish.

1　On the **Layers** tab, click ⊕ **Add Layer**. Rename the new layer 'Curve Text.'

2　Open keyframe 5 in the workspace.

Use the **A Artistic Text** tool to create a text object containing the words 'Arts & Crafts.'

- Click and drag to resize the text to about 15 pts (or use the context toolbar.)

- On the context toolbar, apply a script style font.

- On the **Swatch** tab, apply the **RGB (88, 84, 0)** swatch to the text fill.

- Position the text object just inside the 'dip' of the swish.

3　Select the text object then on the Text context toolbar, click to expand the ✎ **Curved Text** flyout.

- Click the **Bottom Circle** preset curve.

DrawPlus fits your text into a 'U' curve.

4　On the Drawing toolbar, click the ▽ **Node** tool.

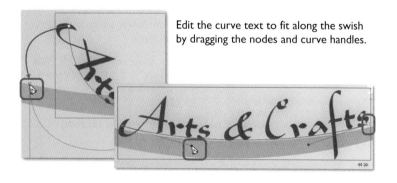

Edit the curve text to fit along the swish by dragging the nodes and curve handles.

5 With the text object selected:

- On the **Colour** tab, set the **Opacity slider** to **50%**.

- Click ▷▷ **Run Forward** and run the text through to the end of the storyboard.

6 Open keyframe 6 and select the curve text object:

- On the **Colour** tab, set the **Opacity slider** to **100%**.

- On the object toolbar, click ▷ **Update attributes forward**.

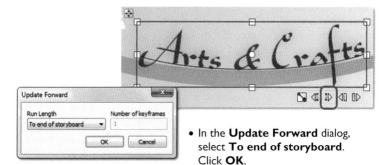

- In the **Update Forward** dialog, select **To end of storyboard**. Click **OK**.

This tells DrawPlus to apply 100% opacity to the remainder of the 'run' of the curve text object. (In this example, there is only one more keyframe in the run.)

7 Preview your animation and make any final adjustments, as required.

When you're happy with your animated banner, you're ready to export it.

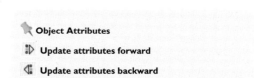

Object Attributes

▷ **Update attributes forward**

◁ **Update attributes backward**

Click to apply a selected object's attributes (fill, line, effects, etc.) to the same object in subsequent or previous keyframes, or to the start or end of the storyboard.

Export to Adobe Shockwave Flash

For this project, we will export our animation to a standard Adobe®
Shockwave Flash® .swf file.

To export as Flash

1   On the **File** menu, point to **Export** and then click **Export as Flash
    SWF…**

2   Choose a file name and save location for your .swf file and then click
    Save.

3   The **Keyframe Animation Export** dialog displays the progress of
    the export and closes when export is complete.

    Simply browse to locate the file and then double-click to open it.

Congratulations, you've reached the end of the project! We hope that you
have enjoyed learning how to use masks in DrawPlus animations. With a
little bit of practise, we're sure you'll soon be using them to create
impressive, dynamic effects.

If you'd like to work through some more step-by-step animation examples,
take a look at the other tutorials in the **Animation & Web** section.

Projects

These projects reinforce the use of multiple tools and provide a problem/solution approach to creative design challenges.

Designing a Garden

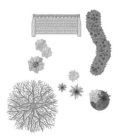

On the **Gallery** tab, in the **Layout Symbols** category, you'll find the **Garden** layout symbols.

This extensive image collection includes garden furniture, buildings, surfaces, paths and borders, as well as a selection of containers, bedding plants, trees, and shrubs.

Simply 'drag and drop' your favourite images onto the page to quickly and easily design beautiful garden layouts.

Follow the steps in this tutorial and learn how to:

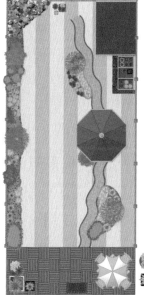

- Scale your drawing to your garden.

- Use ruler guides to help you position objects on the page.

- Place **Garden** symbols on to your page, resizing them where necessary.

- Align and order objects on the page.

You'll find our sample garden layout, **Garden.dpp**, in the ...**Workspace** folder of your DrawPlus installation directory—normally located at:

C:\Program Files\Serif\DrawPlus\X3\Tutorials

Our garden is 6 metres wide by 13 metres long. At the moment, the whole area is grass, but we have big plans! We want to keep a big expanse of lawn; however, we also want to build a summerhouse and a deck/patio area for outdoor eating. We'd love a cold frame, and really need a shed to store bikes and gardening tools. Trouble is, we can't decide where all of these elements should go. Fortunately, we've got DrawPlus to help us out!

Let's start by creating our document and setting up the scale options.

To scale a drawing

1   In the DrawPlus Startup Wizard, choose **Drawing**. Select a Letter or A4 Portrait page size and click **Open**.

Before we begin to design, we need to decide what scale factor to use to fit our garden on to the page. If we set one metre of garden space to equal two centimetres, we can represent our 6 m by 13 m garden in a 12 cm by 26 cm page area.

2   On the Page Context toolbar, click **Options**.

3   In the **Options** dialog, select the **Drawing Scale** option.

- Select the **Scale Drawing** check box.

- Under **Page Distance:** Enter '2,' and select 'centimetres' as the page unit.

- Under **Ruler Distance:** Enter '1,' and select 'metres' as the ruler unit.

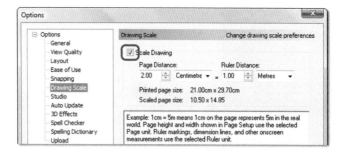

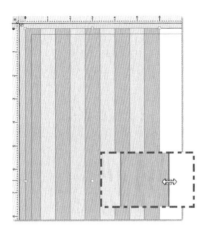

With our page set up to scale we can place our lawn section.

When you design your garden, remember that your drawing will not print right to the edge of the page. To avoid having the printer cut off the edges of the lawn, we need to make sure that it does not extend into the page margins (represented by solid blue lines bordering the page). We'll use ruler guides—non-printing, red lines—to help us position our lawn appropriately.

To position the lawn using ruler guides

1 On the **Gallery** tab, in the category drop-down list, click **Layout Symbols**. Expand the **Garden** category and click **Surfaces and Features**. Scroll down the list of symbols and find **Lawn 9**. Click and drag it over to your page.

2 Resize the lawn to 6 m by 13 m by dragging the size handles.

3 To create a vertical ruler guide, click on the vertical ruler running down the left of the page and drag towards the page. A blue vertical line appears. Drag the line to the 1 metre ruler mark and release the mouse button. A red ruler guide line appears.

   Repeat to place a ruler guide at the 7 metre mark.

4 To create a horizontal rule guide, click on the horizontal ruler running across the top of the page. Drag down to the 1 metre ruler mark and release the mouse button. A red ruler guide line appears.

   Repeat to place a guide at the 14 metre mark.

To move a ruler guide:

Click and drag it—it will follow the current cursor position.

To remove a ruler guide:

Drag and drop it anywhere outside the page area.

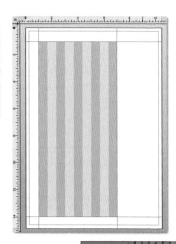

You should now have a 6 m by 13 m area sectioned off with ruler guides.

5   Select your lawn and move it into the area you've just created.

With our lawn scaled and in place, we're ready to build the deck!

To create a garden deck

1   On the **Gallery** tab, still in the **Garden/Surfaces and Features** category, locate **Decking section blue** (or **Decking section natural** if you prefer) and drag it over to your page.

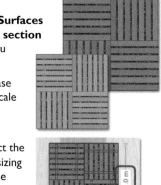

The decking sections we intend to purchase come in 1m x 1m square sections. Let's scale our decking section to match these dimensions.

2   Click the 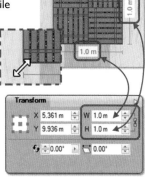 **Pointer** tool and then select the decking section. Click one of the corner sizing handles and drag it to a new position while holding down the left mouse button. Release the mouse button when the decking section measures 1m x 1m (you can also type the dimensions into the **W** (width) and **H** (height) boxes on the **Transform** tab).

We want to build a 6m by 2m deck right across the top of our garden. We can do this by simply cutting and pasting this first section. (You can copy our deck, or create your own if you prefer a different size or shape.)

3 Right click the decking section and click **Copy**. Right-click again and click **Paste**.

A copy of the object is pasted on top of the original and is automatically selected.

To size your garden elements precisely, it will help if you zoom in. To do this, click the Zoom In button— located on the HintLine toolbar.

4 Move the two sections into place at the top of the garden (in our example, this corresponds to the lower edge of the page). Zooming in will help you do this.

5 Draw a selection bounding box around both objects to select the decking sections.

• On the **Align** tab, click **Align Right**.

• Select the **Spaced** option and set it to 0.0m. Click the **Vertical Distribute** button.

The objects are perfectly aligned.

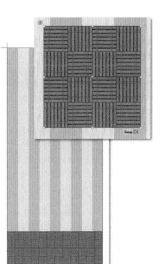

6 With the objects still selected, click Group . Now right-click the new group and click **Copy**. Right-click again and click **Paste**.

7 The copied group is pasted on top of the original and selected by default. Click and drag it into place next to the first two sections.

8 Repeat step 5 to align the four sections, this time clicking Align **Bottom** and Horizontal **Distribute**.

9 Repeat the **Copy**, **Paste**, and **Align** procedures to complete the whole deck.

We're pretty excited about the summerhouse, so let's add this next. We also think it would be nice to build a path leading from the deck to the summerhouse, so we'll 'build' that too...

To create a summerhouse and path

1   On the **Gallery** tab, in the **Garden/Buildings and Fixtures** category, locate **Octagon summerhouse** and drag it on to your page.

2   Resize the summerhouse to the dimensions you want to use—ours is 2.5m wide, and then move it into position in the garden.

If you prefer something simpler, the Gallery also contains a rectangular-shaped summerhouse, called simply '**Summerhouse**.'

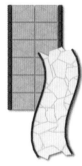

Now for the path. The DrawPlus **Gallery** tab provides a selection of straight and curved path sections to choose from. We think a curved path would look good, but you can choose whichever style you prefer.

3   In the **Garden/Surfaces and Features** category, locate the path section of your choice (we used **Curved path section 1**) and drag it on to your page. Resize the path section by clicking and dragging one of its corner handles. We scaled our path section down to a width of approximately 0.5m.

4   Select the path section, right-click, and then click **Copy**. Right-click again and click **Paste**. A copy of the object is pasted on top of the original and is selected by default. Drag this copy off to the side so that you can see both path sections.

5   On the HintLine toolbar, click the 👤 **Zoom In** button and zoom in on the path sections. Note how they have been designed to allow you to lay them end-to-end.

Now drag the sections into place so that their edges interlock, as illustrated.

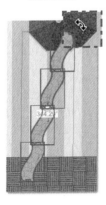

6 Continue copying and pasting the path sections until your path is long enough to stretch between the deck and the summerhouse.

7 Select the entire path, then click the Group 🗗 button. Your path sections are combined into a single object, which you can move and resize with ease.

8 Use the 🖰 **Pointer** tool to drag the path into position. To rotate the path, hover the mouse pointer by a corner handle. When the pointer changes to curved arrow, click and drag to the new angle.

All we need to do now is change the **order of objects** on the page.

9 Click the summerhouse, then on the **Align** tab, click the 🗗 **Bring to Front** button. The end of the path disappears behind the summerhouse object.

10 Now click on the decking section that meets the other end of the path. Again, click the 🗗 **Bring to Front** button to bring the deck to the front of the drawing.

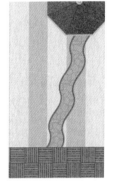

💡 **Object order**

Think of the objects on a page as being stacked on top of each other.

Each time you create a new object, it is placed in front of the objects already on the page.

However, you can move any object to any level in the ordering sequence using the **Arrange** menu's **Order Objects** commands.

For more information, see "Ordering objects" in online Help.

Now that you're familiar with the process of adding objects to your garden layout, and scaling and ordering them on your page, you can go ahead and complete your design.

You don't need us to provide step-by-step instructions. We will, however, show you our finished layout and highlight any tips that we think you'll find useful.

Rockery

We dragged the **Rockery corner** symbol from the **Surfaces and Features** category, then added a variety of plants from the **Hedges, Shrubs, and Trees** category.

Patio

We chose **Patio surface 4** to match the colour of the path. If you don't like our choice, you'll find another five patio surfaces in the **Surfaces and Features** category—along with a selection of other surfaces such as bark chip, coir matting, gravel, and pebble (which we used under the cold frame).

Potted plants

We livened up our deck and patio with a selection of potted plants. You'll find a range of empty containers 'ready for planting' in the **Containers** category.

Cold frame

We decided that a cold frame would be adequate for our needs, and for the size of the garden. If you have bigger ideas, however, you can add one of the greenhouses instead. Don't forget to put a few plants inside for authenticity!

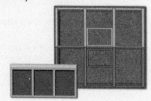

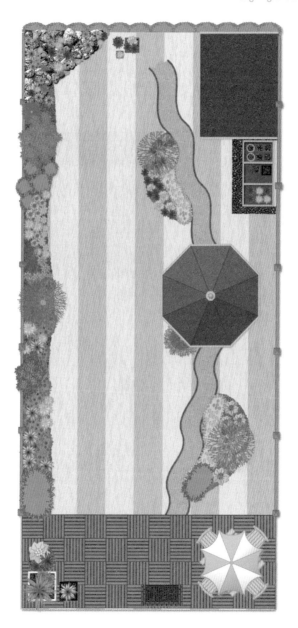

Borders

We used **Border area 2** from the **Surfaces and Features** category for the main border area, then dragged various trees and shrubs on to it.

For the two areas either side of the path, we used **Bedding area 5**, which we resized and rotated to fit the curve of the path.

Before placing our plants and trees, we clicked the **Bring to Front** button to place the path sections on top of the bedding areas.

Garden furniture

You'll find a selection of garden and patio furniture in the **Furniture** category. Choose a style and a finish—we chose natural wood—and then imagine yourself relaxing in style and enjoying your beautiful new garden!

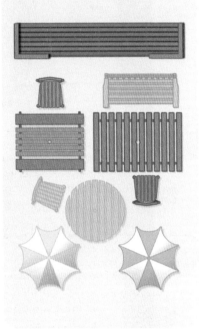

💡 If you have various design ideas in mind, why not create alternative layouts on different layers. You can then hide and display the layers in different combinations and choose your favourite. You can even use the **Layers** tab to locate (and name) your various garden elements, making it easier to work with them.

For instructions on how to create multi-layered documents, see the online Help, or any one of the following tutorials:

- Drawing a Gemstone
- Making a Family Tree

Don't worry—it sounds complicated, but it's really very easy to do!

Creating a Gel Button

If you're an Internet user, you'll no doubt have seen these 'gel' style buttons, in fact, we have even included them in the DrawPlus Gallery. Although they look impressive, they are surprisingly simple to create.

In this tutorial, you'll apply transparency, gradient fills, and filter effects to multi-layered shapes to create striking gel buttons. You'll learn how to:

- Create and manipulate Quick Shapes.

- Use the **Colour** and **Line** tabs to apply properties to a shape.

- Work with gradient transparency.

- Use the **Filter Effects** dialog to apply feather effects.

- Group and ungroup objects.

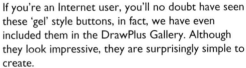

Our gel button samples are provided in the **Gel Buttons.dpp** file, which you'll find in the **...Tutorials\Workspace** folder of your installation directory. In a default installation, this folder is located at:

C:\Program Files\Serif\DrawPlus\X3\Tutorials\Workspace

Our illustration shows what we are aiming to achieve in this tutorial—a translucent gel button with a shadow. We'll show you how simple it is to create this in DrawPlus.

1   In the DrawPlus Startup Wizard, choose **Drawing**, select a page size of your choice and click **Open**.

2   On the left Drawing toolbar, on the Quick Shapes flyout, click the **Quick Rectangle**, then click and drag to draw a large rectangle on your page.

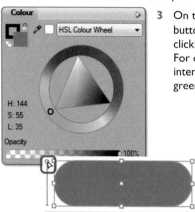

3   On the **Colour** tab, click the **Fill** button, and then apply a fill colour by clicking a point in the colour wheel. For optimum effect, choose a fairly intense colour—we used a mid green.

4   On the **Line** tab, remove the outline from your shape by selecting **None** from the line style drop-down list.

5   Drag the left sliding node all the way up to the top to round the corners fully.

6   Click the **Pointer** tool, then right-click the shape and choose **Copy**. Right-click again and choose **Paste**.

The new shape is pasted on top of the original and is selected by default.

7   On the **Colour** tab, apply a slightly lighter fill colour. (We used **H** 144, **S** 56, **L** 47.)

If you want to create a gel button that you can quickly recolour, try using **linked colours**.

For more information, see the online Help.

8 On the Drawing toolbar, click **Filter Effects**. In the **Filter Effects** dialog, select the **Feather** check box and set the **Blur** value to 10.

Click **OK**.

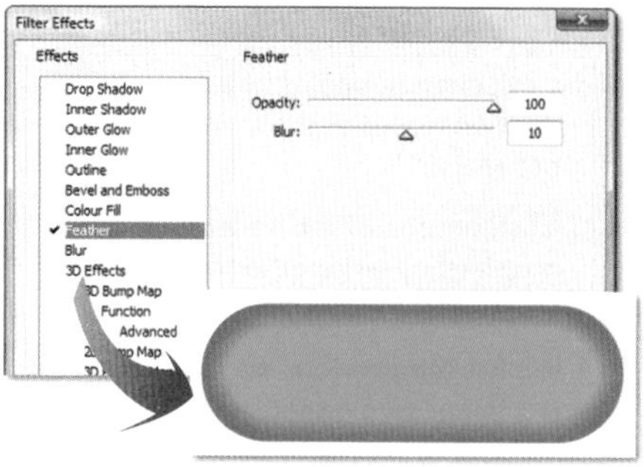

9 Copy and paste this new shape and apply an even lighter colour fill (we used **H** 144, **S** 79, **L** 51). Open the **Filter Effects** dialog again and increase the **Blur** value to 14.

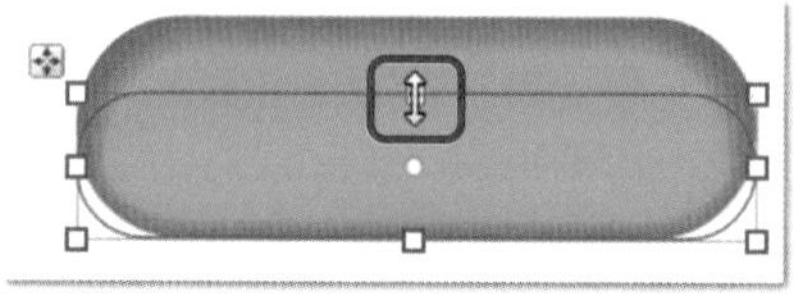

10 With the new rectangle selected, click its upper size handle and drag down to make a thinner shape.

We now have our 'glowing' gel button, but we still need to add a reflection highlight.

Did you know that you can use the **Layers** tab to select objects? Each object has a preview icon that gets larger when you hover over it. With the **Auto Select** button on, when you select an object on the page, it will also be highlighted in the **Layers** tab.

11 Select the original shape and then copy and paste it. Now apply a white fill. This new shape will completely cover the three previous layers.

In order to create our reflection effect, we need to edit this white shape using the **Node** tool. To do this, we must first convert the object to curves.

12 With the white shape selected, on the **Arrange** tab, click **Convert to Curves**.

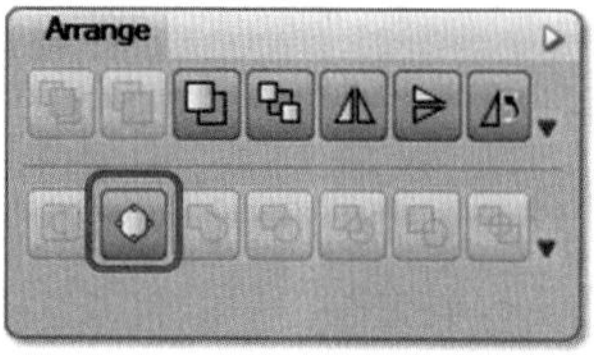

13 Click the 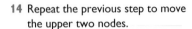 **Node** tool and draw a selection bounding box around the two nodes at the lower edge of the shape.

Click on one of the nodes and drag it up slightly—the other node will also move.

14 Repeat the previous step to move the upper two nodes.

15 Now click the  **Pointer** tool, select the white shape, and reduce its size slightly.

Position the shape in the upper centre area of the button.

Our button looks very effective already. However, with another couple of steps we can make it look even more realistic.

We want to soften the highlight slightly, at the lower edge only. We'll use a gradient transparency to achieve this effect.

16 With the reflection selected, on the Drawing toolbar, click the

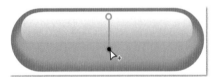

Transparency tool and draw a transparency path from just above to just below the shape.

💡 Transparency effects are great for highlights, shading and shadows, and simulating 'rendered' realism. They can make the critical difference between flat-looking illustrations and images with depth and snap.

Transparency may seem a bit tricky because by definition, you can't see it the way you can see a colour fill applied to an object. In fact, it's there all the time in DrawPlus. Each new object has a transparency property: the default just happens to be 'None'—that is, no transparency (opaque).

Congratulations, you've created your gel button. Now to add a shadow. This is an important step because it gives the button a translucent appearance.

17 Click the ▶ **Pointer** tool and select the original large shape from your button—the easiest way is to select the object on the **Layers** tab. Copy and paste the shape and move it away from the button.

18 On the Drawing toolbar, click 🖈 **Filter Effects**. Select the **Feather** check box and set the **Blur** value to 13.

19 Copy and paste this new shape, make it smaller and lighter in colour, and position it on top of the shadow base. Select both objects and click Group 🔲.

20 Now select your grouped shadow objects and on the **Arrange** tab click 🖳 **Send to Back**. Adjust the size of the shadow if needed.

21 Finally, with the shadow still selected, on the **Colour** tab adjust the **Opacity** of the shadow to 45%.

💡 It's a good idea to 'group' the various objects in your drawing. When objects are grouped, you can position, resize, rotate, or shear them at the same time. The objects that comprise a group are intact, but can also be edited individually.

In our gel button example, we grouped all the shapes that make up the button, and then grouped the two 'shadow' shapes. Once we had moved the shadow into place, we grouped everything together.

To create a group:

• Select the objects you want to group, then to the lower right of the selection, click the Group 🔲 button (or right-click and choose **Group**).

To ungroup (turn a group back into a multiple selection)

• Click the Ungroup 🔲 button (or right-click and choose **Ungroup**).

To edit an object contained within a group:

Press and hold down the **Ctrl** key and then click to select the object.

That's all there is to it! We hope you'll agree that the process of creating this gel button is actually a fairly simple one, but the results are very effective.

Creating a
Torn Paper Effect

In this tutorial, you will combine DrawPlus tools and techniques to make a variety of torn paper effects—including a pirate's treasure map.

You'll learn how to:

- Draw lines and shapes with the **Pencil** tool.
- Combine shapes using the **Subtract** command.
- Use the **Roughen** tool to turn smooth edges into jagged outlines.
- Apply bitmap fills and paper textures.
- Use the **Filter Effects** dialog to create a drop shadow.

1 In the DrawPlus Startup Wizard, click **Drawing**, select a page size of your choice, click **Open**.

2 On the left Drawing toolbar, on the Quick Shapes flyout, click the  **Quick Rectangle**, then draw a large rectangle on your page. This rectangle will be your 'piece of paper.'

3 On the Drawing toolbar, click the 🖉 **Pencil** tool and draw a jagged line to represent the torn edge of the paper (**Figure 1**).

   Continue the line outside the edge of the rectangle (**Figure 2**) and connect the start and end nodes to create a shape.

   When you release the mouse button, your new shape will sit on top of the rectangle, hiding its edge (**Figure 3**).

4 On the **Edit** menu, choose **Select All** (or press **Ctrl + A**) to select both the rectangle and the freehand shape.

5 On the **Arrange** tab, click the 🔲 **Subtract** button. DrawPlus removes the section of the rectangle that is overlapped by the freehand shape (**Figure 4**).

🖋 The 🖉 **Pencil** tool uses a cursor with different states to help you to connect nodes and create shapes:

- 🖉 Shows that the **Pencil** tool is selected and that you can draw a line.

- 🖉₊ Shows that you can extend a selected line from an end node.

- 🖉₀ Shows that you can close the shape by joining the line to the starting node.

- 🖉～ Shows that you can change the current path or shape of the line from a mid-point. To do so, select the line and then hover over the section you want to change. When the 🖉～ cursor appears, click and drag to draw the new line shape. You must connect the new path back to the existing line. Release the mouse button when you see the cursor again. Your line will be updated to the new shape.

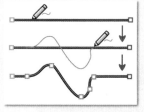

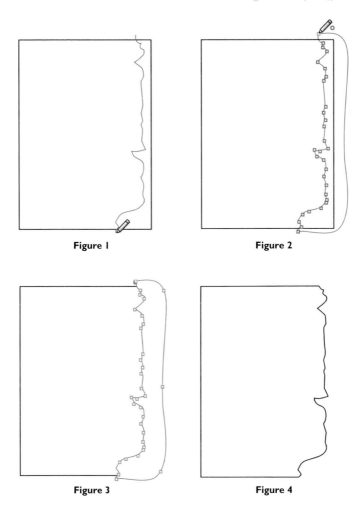

Figure 1

Figure 2

Figure 3

Figure 4

Now that we've got the basic outline for our piece of torn paper, there are a multitude of things we can do with it. We'll show you a few examples then we'll let you experiment on your own...

Curve Smoothness controls

These display in the **Context toolbar** when you select the **Pencil** tool (click the arrow to the right of the value box to display the slider). Use these controls to refine the curve most recently drawn with the **Pencil** tool (as long as the line is still selected).

- Increase the value in the box, or drag the slider to the right, to simplify the line by decreasing the number of nodes. The fewer the nodes, the more the resulting line will deviate from the original line drawn.

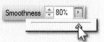

- Decrease the value in the box, or drag the slider to the left, to make the curve more complex by increasing the number of nodes. The greater the number of nodes, the more closely the resulting line will be to the original line drawn

The more nodes there are on a line or shape, the more control you have over the shape. The fewer nodes there are, the simpler (smoother) the line or shape.

Example 1: Newspaper

To achieve this effect we applied one of DrawPlus's predefined bitmap fills to the shape, and then added a drop-shadow.

To apply a bitmap fill

1   Select the shape, and then on the **Swatch** tab, click the ◗▾ **Bitmap** category drop-down list and choose **Misc**.

2   Click the **misc06** swatch to apply it to your shape.

3   On the **Line** tab, click ⊞ **None** to remove the shape's outline.

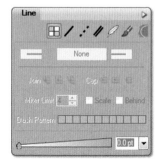

To create a drop shadow

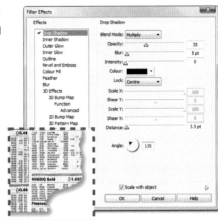

1 Right-click the shape and select **Filter Effects**.

2 In the **Filter Effects** dialog, select the **Drop Shadow** check box and then set the following values:

- **Opacity**: 35
- **Blur**: 5
- **Distance**: 3.5
- **Angle**: 135

Click **OK**.

Example 2: Marbled

Simple but effective, this marbled effect was created by applying and editing a plasma fill.

We also removed the outline and applied a drop shadow.

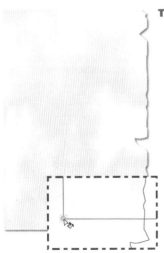

To apply and edit a plasma fill

1 Select the shape and then click the **Swatch** tab.

2 On the **Swatch** tab, in the **Gradient** category drop-down list, choose **Plasma**.

3 Apply any gradient fill by clicking its swatch.

4 With the shape still selected, on the Drawing toolbar, click the **Fill** tool. The shape's fill path and nodes display.

5 On the **Swatch** tab, replace the colours of the fill by dragging from a colour swatch to the nodes.

Example 3: Rough edge

The simplest method of all—we quickly roughened the edge of this piece of paper using the **Roughen** tool. Again, we completed the effect with a drop shadow.

1 Select the shape, remove its outline, and apply the fill of your choice.

2 On the Drawing toolbar, click the
   🔲 **Roughen** tool, then click on your shape and drag either upwards or downwards. The further you drag, the more pronounced the effect. As soon as you release the mouse button, the effect will be applied.

🔖 Only the outline of the shape is affected and there's no internal distortion—so if you have applied a bitmap fill, for example, the fill remains intact.

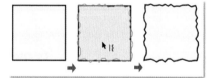

To remove a roughen effect from an object, double-click it with the **Roughen** tool, or click **Remove Roughen Effect** on the context toolbar.

Example 4: Treasure map

Our final example is a pirate's treasure map, which we created using a variety of DrawPlus tools and features. We'll explain how we did it; however, rather than replicating our example, you should have fun with this and explore your own ideas.

You'll find our map, **Treasure Map.dpp**, in the **...\Workspace** folder of your DrawPlus installation, normally located in:

C:\Program Files\Serif\DrawPlus\X3\Tutorials

The individual elements are on **Layer 2** of the treasure map—you'll need to make **Layer 2** visible and the active layer.

Burnt edge effect

We wanted the edges of our map to look charred. To accomplish this, in the **Filter Effects** dialog, we added an **Inner Glow** using the following settings:

Blend Mode: Multiply

Opacity: 75

Blur: **40.5** pt

Intensity: 15

Colour: Mid brown—RGB(128, 80, 47)

Trees

We drew our fir and palm trees with the **Pencil** tool.

We drew the first tree, applied colour and a drop shadow, then we used copy and paste to replicate the original, resizing where necessary.

Caves

For the cave entrances, we used the **Pencil** tool, connecting the start and end nodes to make a closed shape. We then applied a gradient fill to the shapes.

Pirate Ship

A combination of shapes, lines, and fills was used to create our pirate ship.

River and paths

These were drawn with the 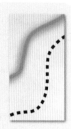 **Pen** tool.

- The river is a simple curved line, with a weight of 7.5 pt.
- We applied drop shadow and feather filter effects to soften the edges.
- For the footpaths, we simply changed the line style to a dotted line on the **Line** tab.

Dragon

Our friendly dragon was created with the **Pencil** tool.

Flowers

We made these with simple **Quick Petals**.

The stalks were drawn with the **Straight Line** tool, and the leaves are **Quick Ellipses**.

Fish

We used the **Pencil** tool for the body, and a **Quick Ellipse** for the eye.

Tents

We used the  **Straight Line** tool to draw the campsite.

Mountains

We used the **Pencil** tool to draw the mountain range. The snowy peaks were created as separate objects. We applied a drop shadow filter effect to each element to create a 3D effect.

Other suggestions...

DrawPlus provides you with a number of other fills and textures that are particularly suitable for creating paper effects.

On the Layers tab:

- Click 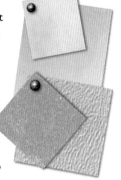 **Apply Paper Texture**, then choose from the wide selection of textures available in the **Bitmap Selector** dialog.

On the Swatch tab:

- Click the **Gradient** category drop-down list and experiment with the **Plasma**, **Four Colour**, and **Three Colour** categories. You can create very different results just by editing the colours and the gradient of the fill path, and adjusting transparency.

- Click the **Bitmap** category drop-down list and explore the **Bitmap/Material** category.

  Try applying various fills, then on the **Transparency** tab, reduce the opacity to 50% to create an interesting paper texture.

Finally, why not try combining fills *and* effects for some really unique paper textures—don't forget to adjust the transparency setting too!

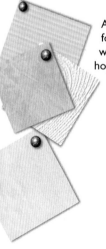

As you can see, once you have created the basic template for your torn paper, there are many things you can do with it. This tutorial has illustrated a few ideas, but we hope it has also inspired you to explore some of your own.

Designing a
Cartoon Movie Poster

The poster—the oldest medium of all—has become an integral part of our society. Its functions are many and include publicity, promotion, advertising, communication, selling, as well as decoration.

However, before it can do any of the above, the first objective of any poster is to attract the attention of its audience.

In this tutorial we'll discuss the various elements of poster design—layout, typeface, graphics, and so on, and show you how to combine these elements into an effective layout. You'll learn how to:

- Lay out a poster publication.
- Use colour effectively in a layout.
- Position and align text and graphics objects.
- Use a variety of typefaces to create different effects.
- Adjust letter spacing.
- Apply gradient fills, filter effects, and perspective.
- Draw a cartoon character using basic Quick Shapes.
- Set up page and printer options.
- Use tiling and scaling to print your poster on multiple pages.

For our fictitious movie, 'Catboy,' we wanted to create a crisp, clean cartoon-style poster.

- For maximum visual impact, we chose blue and orange (complementary colours) along with black and white.

- To keep the layout simple, we kept graphics to a minimum and let the text do most of the work.

- The chunky style of the title text is contrasted with the simpler text style used for the copy line and the credits.

- The copy line "Mischief is coming" and the single image of the main character give the audience a clue as to the movie's genre.

The following pages provide step-by-step instructions to recreate our Catboy poster.

To create the gradient background

1   In the DrawPlus Startup Wizard, choose **Drawing**, select an **A4** or **Letter Portrait** size page and click **Open**.

2   On the Drawing toolbar, on the QuickShapes flyout, click the **Quick Rectangle**. Click in the upper left corner of the page, hold down the mouse button and then drag out a large rectangle to almost fill your page. (We left a 0.4 cm border between the rectangle and the page edge.)

3   On the Drawing toolbar click the **Fill** tool. Click and drag a fill path from the upper right corner to the lower left corner.

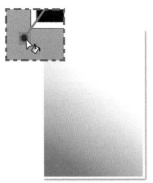

4   On the **Swatch** tab, locate a mid blue swatch, then click and drag it over to the black node at the bottom of the fill path.

(You can also click the node first, and then click the swatch you want to apply.)

5   Now that we have created the background for our poster, we can create the individual elements to place on it. Let's start with the main element—the movie title.

To create the title text

1   On the Drawing toolbar, click the **A** **Artistic Text** tool, then click anywhere outside the blue rectangle and type the word 'catboy.'

2   Double-click the text to select the whole word.

On the Text context toolbar:

- In the font name drop-down list, select a plain, heavy, sans-serif font.

- In the font size list, choose **200 pt**.

3   Just outside the upper-left corner of the text object, click on the ⊹ **Move** button and drag the text to reposition it on the page.

Now for some colour... We'll begin by applying a simple gradient fill to add depth to our title.

4   Select the text object, then click the ◈ **Fill** tool and draw a vertical line through the title from top to bottom.

5   On the **Swatch** tab, click a brown swatch (we used **RGB(128, 80, 47)**) and then drag it over to the node at the bottom of the fill path.

Note: We dragged the top node up to reduce the amount of black in the text fill.

6   Click the 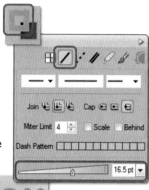 **Pointer** tool and then
    click the text object. On the **Swatch**
    tab, click the **Line** button and then
    click an orange swatch.

7   On the **Line** tab, select a solid line and
    increase the line thickness to 16.5 pt.

    Our title is starting to come together,
    but there are still a few things we can
    do to improve it. Next, we'll reduce the
    letter spacing.

8   With the text object
    selected, click the
    Node tool.
    Adjustment sliders and
    handles appear. The
    rightmost node is the
    Letter slider, click and
    drag this node to the left
    until the letters of the title
    touch.

You'll notice that some of the letters overlap a little too much. Don't
worry, we can easily correct this by adjusting the 'offset'—the spacing of
individual letters.

9   Click on the node to the left of the letter 't,'
    then drag it slightly to the right until the 'a' and
    't' just touch.

10 Repeat this step to adjust the remaining letters.

    Let's now add the final touches—perspective and
    filter effects.

11 With the text object selected, on the Drawing toolbar, click the
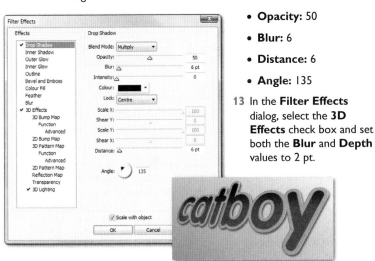 **Perspective** tool. The ▽ **Node** tool becomes the active tool
and an adjustment slider appears
above the object.

• Click and drag directly on the
text with the **Node** tool, which
displays a 3D cursor.

- or -

• Drag the adjustment slider to
customize the effect.

12 On the Drawing toolbar, click ⭐ **Filter Effects**. In the **Filter
Effects** dialog, select the **Drop Shadow** check box and set the
following values:

• **Opacity:** 50

• **Blur:** 6

• **Distance:** 6

• **Angle:** 135

13 In the **Filter Effects**
dialog, select the **3D
Effects** check box and set
both the **Blur** and **Depth**
values to 2 pt.

Congratulations—your movie title is complete!

Let's now move on and create the star of the show—the one and only
Catboy!

You don't need to be an artist to create our cartoon character—you'll be pleased to know that he is very easily constructed from a few basic Quick Shapes.

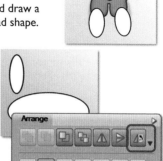

To draw Catboy

1   On the Drawing toolbar, on the Quick Shapes flyout, click the **Quick Ellipse** and draw a wide flattened ellipse for the basic head shape.

2   Repeat the process to draw a small elongated ear shape.

3   Select the small shape and then on the **Arrange** tab, select 45° from the **Rotate** drop-down menu.

4   With the shape still selected, right-click and choose **Copy**. Then right-click again and choose **Paste**.

A copy of the shape is pasted directly on top of the original and is selected by default.

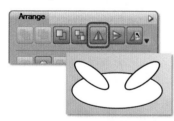

5   On the **Arrange** tab, click **Flip Horizontal t**o flip the copied shape. Now drag the two shapes into position, as illustrated.

6   Click the **Pointer** tool and then draw a selection bounding box around the three ellipses to select them all (or click one shape, then hold down the **Shift** key and click on the others to add them to the selection).

7   On the **Arrange** tab, click **Add** to combine the shapes.

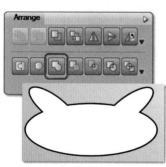

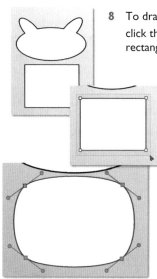

8 To draw the body, on the QuickShapes flyout, click the □▾ **Quick Rectangle** and draw a rectangle under the head shape.

9 On the **Arrange** tab, click ○ **Convert to Curves**.

10 Click the ▽ **Node** tool. A node displays in each corner of the rectangle. Click and drag around the outside of the rectangle to select all of these nodes.

11 On the Curve context bar, click the ⌃ **Smart Corner** button to round the corners of your shape.

12 Repeat step 4 to copy and paste the rounded rectangle. We'll use this shape for Catboy's arm—resize it and move it into place, then repeat the copy and paste process to create the other arm.

13 Repeat the previous step to create the legs.

14 Select the body, arms, and legs shapes and then on the **Arrange** tab, click 🕭 **Add** to combine them.

15 With the body selected, on the **Swatch** tab, click the **Fill** button and then click a blue swatch to apply a blue fill to the shape (we used **RGB(92, 188, 252)**).

16 Create five more ellipses for Catboy's hands, feet, and hood.

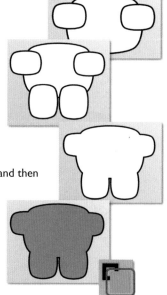

17 To flatten the top of the hood, convert the shape to curves and then drag the top node down a little, as illustrated.

Next, we'll create the tail with a freeform shape:

18 On the Drawing toolbar, click the  **Freeform Paint** tool.

- On the context toolbar, set the **Width** to 8.

- On the **Swatch** tab, set the **Fill** to white and the outline to black.

Click where you want the shape to start, and hold the mouse button down as you draw.

The shape appears immediately and follows your mouse movements. To complete the shape, release the mouse button.

19 Click the 📝 **Pencil** tool use it to draw the whiskers.

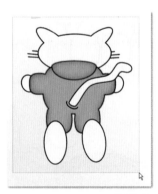

20 Press and hold down the **Alt** key, then use the 🔻 **Pointer** tool to draw a selection bounding box around Catboy.

To the lower right of the selection, click Group 🔄 .

💡 When selecting objects that are positioned on top of another object—in this case the blue gradient background—holding down the **Alt** key allows you begin drawing the selection box over the background object without including it in the multiple selection.

21 On the Drawing toolbar, click **Filter Effects** (or right-click the Catboy figure and choose **Filter Effects**).

In the **Filter Effects** dialog, select the **Drop Shadow** check box and set the following values:

- **Opacity:** 12
- **Blur:** 3.8
- **Distance:** 19.5
- **Angle:** 270

Click **OK**.

22 That's it, Catboy is complete! Just use the 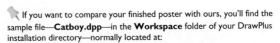 **Pointer** tool to drag him into position.

The remaining elements of the poster are very simple to create. Rather than breaking them down into step-by-step procedures, we'll briefly summarize each element instead. We'll list the tools and settings we used, and point out any specific design considerations where applicable.

If you want to compare your finished poster with ours, you'll find the sample file—**Catboy.dpp**—in the **Workspace** folder of your DrawPlus installation directory—normally located at:

C:\Program Files\Serif\DrawPlus\X3\Tutorials

To create the scratches

1 We first drew a line with the **Pencil** tool and applied a mid-grey colour.

2 With the line selected, we used the **Roughen** tool to create a jagged effect.

Once we were happy with our first set of scratches, we grouped them, and then copied and pasted the group to create the second set.

Note the centre alignment of the credit text lines. This symmetry is a nice contrast to the position of the other elements of our poster.

For the 'summer 2008' line we are continuing a theme by echoing the same font style used in the title text, only at 21 pt as opposed to 200 pt.

The credit lines are in **7 pt Times New Roman**—a traditional serif font. When using small text, it's advisable to use a serif font to maximize readability.

We wanted a clean, 'sans-serif' font for the copy line and decided on **60 pt Arial Black**.

This font style contrasts sharply with the title text and is a perfect fit for the black-outlined cartoon-style graphic.

The size is big enough to grab attention, but not so big that it overpowers the layout.

Congratulations! You have finished your poster and are ready to print it out!

In the following section, we'll discuss the various printing options available in DrawPlus.

Printing your poster

Our sample poster was created on a standard A4 paper size. However, posters and banners are often large-format documents where the page size extends across multiple sheets of paper. To have DrawPlus take care of the printing, set up your document beforehand. You can do this in one of the following ways:

- From the DrawPlus Startup Wizard, click **Start New Drawing**, select the **Large Publications** option, then choose from one of the preset templates.

  - or -

- In DrawPlus, click **File** then click **Page Setup**. In the **Page Setup** dialog, choose the **Large** option and select from the drop-down list of templates.

Tiling and scaling

If your document isn't set up as a poster or banner, you can use tiling and scaling settings to print large (or enlarged) pages using multiple sheets of paper. Each section or tile is printed on a single sheet of paper, and the various tiles can then be joined to form the complete page. To simplify arrangement of the tiles and to allow for printer margins, you can specify an overlap value.

To print a poster or banner from a standard page

1 In the **Print** dialog, click the **Layout** tab.

2 On the **Layout** tab:

- In the **Special Printing** section, select the **As in document** option and then set the **% Scale factor**.

- In the **Tiling** section, select the **Print tiled pages** option, and then set the **Tile overlap** required (to allow for printer margins).

To the right of the **Layout** tab, the preview shows you how many pages will be required to print the document.

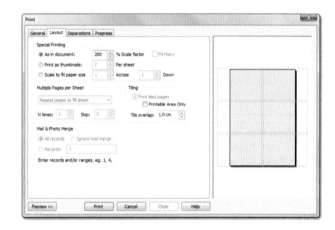

Generating professional output

There may be times when you want a professional printer to output your DrawPlus document. For example:

- If you need to reproduce more than about 500 copies (photocopying begins to lose its economic advantages at this point).

- If you need spot colour or process colour printing for a particular job.

The **Print** dialog's **Prepress** tab allows you set special options such as bleed limit, crop marks, and so on.

For more information, see the "Setting prepress options" topic in online Help.

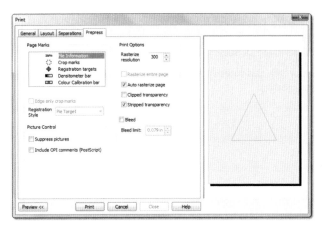

PostScript® files

A standard way of delivering a desktop document to a commercial printer or service bureau is to generate one or more **PostScript® files** that can be passed along on disk or via modem to the bureau.

For detailed information and instructions, see the "Generating professional output" topic in online Help.

Why not have your movie poster or cartoon character printed on a novelty item such as a T-shirt, mouse pad. or mug.

With DrawPlus you can export your design to various file formats, such as JPEG or TIFF. You can also change settings such as file size and resolution.

Contact your local print shop to find out the exact file specifications they require to print a particular item.

PDF files

Another option for delivering files to a bureau or commercial printer is Adobe's **Portable Document Format** (PDF). PDF is increasingly used to distribute documents as electronic 'replicas' over the Web. Anyone using Adobe's Acrobat Reader, regardless of their computer platform, can view and/or print out your document in its original form.

For details on exporting your DrawPlus documents to PDF format, see the "Exporting PDF files" topic in online Help.

Hopefully, this tutorial has given you some ideas, now all you need to do is get creating!

Making a Family Tree

On the DrawPlus **Gallery** tab, you'll find an extensive collection of predefined objects—symbols, shape art, text art, logos, and so on—that you can use in your drawings. The various objects are divided into categories, which are displayed in a drop-down list at the top of the **Gallery** tab.

In this tutorial, we'll introduce you to the Gallery's **Family Tree** category.

You'll learn how to:

- Place symbols from the Gallery on to your page.
- Group, ungroup, and align objects.
- Use the **Connector** tool.
- Import, resize, and crop photographs.
- Make adjustments to image brightness and contrast, and enhance vintage photographs.
- Edit and format text objects.
- Add a background texture.
- Work with layers and transparency.

- In the DrawPlus Startup Wizard, choose **Start New Drawing**, select a 'Portrait' page size of your choice and click **Open**.

To create the tree structure

1 On the right of the workspace, click the **Gallery** tab, and then in the category drop-down list expand the **Connecting Symbols/Family Tree/Photographic** category to display the various symbols available.

   Click on the **Single Photo Frame** symbol, drag it over to the left side of your page and then release the mouse button.

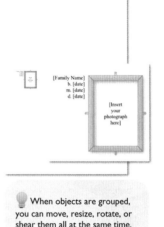

2 Select the text box inside the photo frame and press the **Delete** key.

3 Select the frame and remaining text box by drawing a selection bounding box around them. Click the Group button below the selection.

💡 When objects are grouped, you can move, resize, rotate, or shear them all at the same time.

4 On the **Align** tab, click 🔲 **Centre Vertically**.

5 With the frame and text box group still selected, press and hold the **Ctrl** key and then drag away to create a copy of the group.

6 Position the copied group above and to the right of the original group.

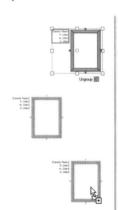

7 With the new copy still selected, hold down the **Ctrl** key and then drag another copy down, keeping it vertically aligned with the second group by holding down the **Shift** key.

   If you need to adjust the position of your groups, you can align them at any stage by using the **Align** tab.

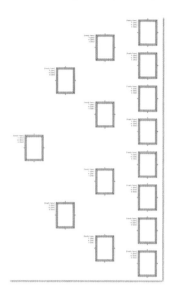

💡 To space objects evenly on a page, vertically or horizontally, select all the objects and then in the **Align Objects** dialog, select the **Space Evenly** option.

8 Repeat the **Ctrl** + drag procedure to create and position an additional 12 photo frame objects.

Your finished structure should resemble our illustration, right.

Our next task is to connect the photo frames. We'll use the **Connector** tool to do this, but before we do so, we need to break up the photo frame and text box groups (remember we grouped them earlier in step 3).

9 To ungroup, select any frame and text box object then click Ungroup 🔲 . Repeat this step for each frame group.

💡 You can also group and ungroup objects by clicking the 🔲 **Group/Ungroup** button on the **Arrange** tab.

10 On the Drawing toolbar, on the Line tools flyout, click the 🔲 **Connector** tool. On the context toolbar, the Connector controls and buttons are now displayed.

11 On the context toolbar, click the 🔲 **Right Angle Connector** tool.

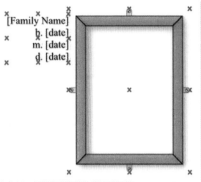

Hover the cursor over a frame to display its **connection points**.

These default connection points can't be moved or deleted, but you can create additional ones if required. For more information, see online Help.

12 Starting with the leftmost photo frame, click on its upper connection point and then drag to the left connection point of the frame above it.

Repeat this procedure to connect each photo frame to each of its two 'parent' frames.

Your finished structure should resemble ours.

Congratulations! You've completed the basic 'tree' structure of your family tree. Now it's time to add the photographs and personal details for each of your family members.

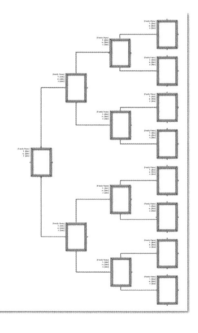

To import and crop a photograph

1   On the Drawing toolbar, click the ▣ **Insert Picture** button.

In the **Insert Picture**
dialog, browse to locate
the photograph you
want to import, click to
select the file, and then
click **Open**.

The dialog disappears
and the mouse pointer
changes to the
⊹▣ **Picture Import**
cursor.

What you do next
determines the initial
size, placement, and aspect
ratio (proportions) of the image.

- To insert the picture at a default size, simply click the mouse.

- or -

- To set the size of the inserted picture, drag out a region and release
  the mouse button. Normally, the picture's aspect ratio is preserved.

Unless you're lucky, your photograph won't fit exactly inside the photo
frame. Don't worry though, with DrawPlus you can crop an image to
any size. Let's do this now...

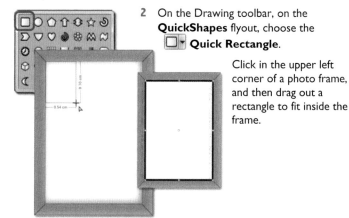

2   On the Drawing toolbar, on the
    QuickShapes flyout, choose the
    ▣▾ **Quick Rectangle**.

    Click in the upper left
    corner of a photo frame,
    and then drag out a
    rectangle to fit inside the
    frame.

3   On the **Colour** tab, click the small **No Fill** button to make the shape transparent.

4   Drag the rectangle into position on top of your photograph.

5   Now select both the photograph and the **Quick Rectangle**.

On the **Arrange** tab, in the **Crop** drop-down list, click **Crop to Top**.

6   Now drag your photo inside its photo frame—it should fit perfectly.

Now that you've imported your first photo, you can repeat these steps to add the rest of your family photos to your family tree.

If you're working with old or less-than-perfect photos, you might want to improve the image quality, or apply a similar style to all of the photos.

Note that any image adjustments must be made before cropping your photographs.

DrawPlus includes some powerful image adjustment tools that enable you to adjust images after importing them.

To learn more, see "Making image adjustments" later in this tutorial.

If you are happy with the quality of your imported photographs, however, you can move right on to the next section.

With all your photos in place, it's time to put your family members' details into the text boxes. The photo frame template we are using in this exercise provides placeholders for family name, date of birth, marriage, and death, but you can add any information you want.

> [Family Name]
> b. [date]
> m. [date]
> d. [date]

To add family member details

1   With the  **Pointer** tool, click any text box to select it. On the Text context toolbar, select the font size and style you want to use.

| A | 📄 | Times New Roman | ▼ | 6 pt | ▼ | **B** | *I* | U | ≡ ≡ ≡ ≡ |

2   On the HintLine toolbar, click 🔼 **Zoom In** to zoom into the area you're working on.

3   Click the **A** **Artistic Text** tool, then click and drag to select all of the text inside the text box.

Replace the placeholder text with your family member's details.

Well done, you've completed your family tree!

At this point, you could simply add a title to your masterpiece (using the **A** **Artistic Text** tool), and then print it out.

However, if you'd like to add some creative flair and interest to your family tree, we've got a few ideas to inspire you...

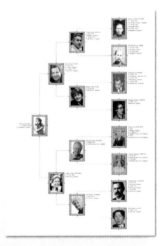

🔖 Note that in our family tree we added the place of birth, marriage, and death (where applicable).

We also moved the text boxes to the right of the photo frames, and changed the text alignment by selecting each text box and then clicking the **Align Left** button on the Text context toolbar.

Robert Charles DAVIES
b. 2 Sept 1915
in Croydon, Surrey, England
m. 10 Jun 1945
in Cardiff, Wales
d. 22 Dec 2003
in Brighton, England

Example 1: Applying an effect from the Effects tab

DrawPlus provides you with a wide range of preset effects that you can apply to any filled shape, including text. Once you've applied an effect, you can customize it and then add it to the **Effects** tab—making it available to use again. For more information, see online Help.

To apply an effect

1   Draw a ▭▾ **Quick Rectangle** the size of the page and place it behind your family tree structure by clicking **Arrange/Order Objects/Send to Back**. On the **Colour** tab, apply any colour fill to the shape.

2   With the rectangle selected, click the **Effects** tab and choose **Wood** from the drop-down category list. Click the **Basswood** thumbnail to apply it.

3   On the **Colour** tab, set the **Opacity Slider** to apply the desired opacity value.

Example 2: Applying a paper texture

With DrawPlus paper textures you can quickly and easily add an interesting textured background to your creations. Here's how we did it...

To apply a paper texture

1   Draw a ▭▾ **Quick Rectangle** the size of your page and place it behind the family tree structure.

2   With the shape selected, on the **Swatch** tab apply a mid pink colour—we used RGB(255, 218, 218).

3   On the **Layers** tab, click the ▫ **Apply Paper Texture** button.

4   In the **Bitmap Selector** dialog, choose the **Abstract** category, click the **Bitmap Swatch 4** swatch, and then click **OK** to apply it to the page.

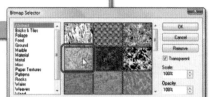

Example 3: Creating a background image

For something really unique, why not add a watermark effect to your family tree. You can use any image or photograph for this, and the process is very simple.

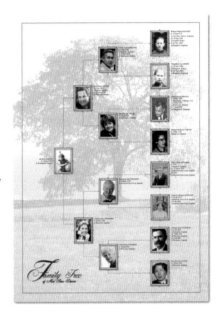

In our example, we used a photograph of a tree. Equally effective would be an image that holds some special significance for your family. The following steps explain how we achieved this effect by creating a new layer in our document.

To create a background image

1   On the **Layers** tab, click the ✛ **Add Layer** button. The new layer (Layer 2) displays at the top of the **Layers** tab list and is selected by default.

2   With the new layer still selected, on the **Layers** tab click the ▽ **Move Layer Down** button. This places Layer 2 behind Layer 1 in your document.

3   Let's temporarily hide Layer 1 so that we can concentrate on our Layer 2 image.

4 On the **Layers** tab, click the  **Hide/Show Layer** button for Layer 1.

Your family tree disappears (don't worry, it's only temporary—click the **Hide/Show Layer** button again if you don't believe us!), leaving you with a blank page displayed.

5 Click the 🖼 **Insert Picture** button and import your image, resizing it so that it fills your page.

6 With the image selected, on the **Colour** tab, use the **Opacity slider** to apply 26% opacity.

7 Finally, click the 👁 **Hide/Show Layer** button to display Layer 1 on top of Layer 2.

💡 Try creating a range of different background images and textures, each on different layers. You can then experiment with various effects by displaying different combinations of layers.

Making image adjustments

In the next section we'll demonstrate how to use the new **Image Adjustments** dialog to enhance your images. Keep in mind, however, that because all photographs are unique, you may have to experiment with various adjustments and settings to achieve results you are happy with.

Correcting bright and dark photographs

Too bright or too dark photographs are fairly common, so this adjustment is one you'll probably end up using quite often.

To adjust image brightness and contrast

1 Import the required image. Notice that the **Picture context toolbar** displays.

2   With the image selected, click the **Image Adjustments** button.

3   In the **Image Adjustments** dialog, click the **Add Adjustment**
    button and then select **Brightness and Contrast**.

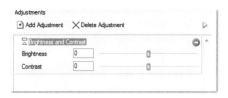

4   Adjust the image brightness and contrast by dragging the sliders.

    The **Image Preview** pane updates to show the effects of your
    adjustments.

    When you are happy with your results, click **OK**.

Enhancing vintage photographs

For our family tree example, we imported a number of vintage
photographs. Old photos tend to vary greatly in quality and this is one area
in which you'll need to experiment with the various image adjustment
tools. Bear in mind that you will only achieve a certain level of
improvement—you will not get a perfect finished result, but you should be
able to enhance the image significantly. The following steps describe how
we enhanced one of our photos.

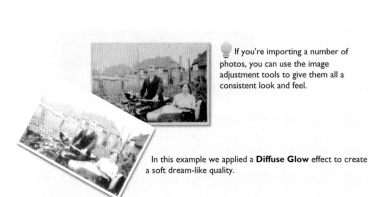

If you're importing a number of
photos, you can use the image
adjustment tools to give them all a
consistent look and feel.

In this example we applied a **Diffuse Glow** effect to create
a soft dream-like quality.

To enhance a vintage photograph

1   Import the required image and with the image selected, click the **Image Adjustments** button.

2   In the **Image Adjustments** dialog, click the **Add Adjustment** button and then select **Brightness and Contrast**.

💡 You can use the Picture context toolbar for some image adjustments—applying transparency, adjusting brightness and contrast, adjusting levels, and fixing red eye.

Adjust the image brightness and contrast by dragging the sliders or typing directly into the boxes. (We reduced brightness and increased contrast.)

3   Click the **Add Adjustment** button again and select **Hue/Saturation/Lightness**.

Adjust the values. (We increased hue and reduced saturation.)

4   Experiment with the other adjustments and when you are happy with your results, click **OK** to apply them.

🔎 The DrawPlus image adjustment tools provide you with the means to enhance your images and correct minor imperfections.

However, to correct more severe flaws—rips, scratches, and so on—you'll need to use photo-editing software such as Serif PhotoPlus.

Drawing a Gemstone

In this tutorial, we'll make use of layers to keep different sections of our drawing intact. We'll also be combining various DrawPlus tools and techniques so if you're a new user, you might want to try some of the earlier tutorials before beginning this one.

In particular, it will help if you are somewhat familiar with layers and with line tools and node editing— we'll outline the basic principles here, but for more detailed information see online Help.

In this exercise, you will:

- Work with the **Layers** tab.
- Use QuickShapes and lines to create custom shapes.
- Use the **Node** tool to edit lines and shapes.
- Apply gradient fills.
- Create custom fills and add them to the DrawPlus Gallery.
- Apply transparency.

The gemstone design we're going to create is fairly complex, so this tutorial is an ideal opportunity to work with layers. Before we begin, let's go over some basic concepts...

By default, all new DrawPlus documents consist of a single layer. Objects created on this layer are stacked in order, from back to front, with each new object in front of the others. For simple designs, one layer is usually sufficient, but if you're working on a complex design it makes sense to separate groups of objects on different layers. This allows you to work on one layer at a time without disturbing elements on other layers.

The **Layers** tab displays all the layers in a document and their properties (you can turn these on or off by clicking the appropriate button). The hierarchical tree view displays thumbnail previews of the objects on each layer.

- To display the objects contained on a layer, click the + sign to the left of the layer to expand it.

- To see a larger preview of an object, hover over a thumbnail preview.

- To select an object on the page, click it's thumbnail.

- The coloured line under each layer's properties buttons indicates the colour of the selection 'bounding box' of all objects on this layer. In our illustration, selected objects on **Layer 1** display with a blue selection bounding box; objects on **Layer 2** display with a red bounding box.

- Use the buttons at the bottom of the **Layers** tab to add and delete layers, change the layer order, edit all, and/or view all layers.

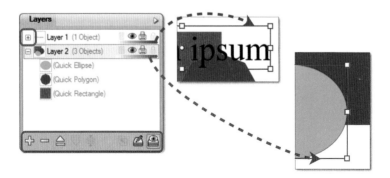

You'll find our sample file—**Gem.dpp**—in the **...\Workspace** folder of your DrawPlus installation, which is normally located at:

C:\Program Files\Serif\DrawPlus\X3\Tutorials

The file consists of four layers:

Layers 1, 2, and 3 form the finished gemstone. You will create your own versions of these layers in this tutorial.

Layer 4 illustrates the various stages involved in the creation of the gemstone. This layer is hidden by default so you'll need to make it visible.

You'll learn more about layers as you work through this exercise, so let's get started.

To create a document and add layers

1   In the DrawPlus Startup Wizard, choose **Drawing**, select a page size of your choice and click **Open**.

2   On the **Layers** tab, right-click **Layer 1** and select **Layer Properties**.

    In the **Layer Properties** dialog, in the **Name:** box, type 'Pavilion' and click **OK**.

    (To change the colour of the selection bounding box for this layer, click the colour swatch to open the **Colour Picker**.)

3   On the **Layers** tab, click the ⊕ **Add Layer** button. Name this second layer 'Crown' and click **OK**.

4   Repeat the previous step to add a third layer named 'Table.'

    Your layers should be in the same sequence as ours. If they're not, you can reorder them by clicking on a layer, and then clicking ⊜ **Move Layer Up** or ⊽ **Move Layer Down**.

5   On the **File** menu, click **Save** and save your document as **Gem.dpp**.

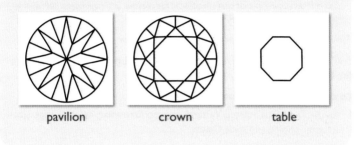

Gem nomenclature

If you're wondering why we've named our layers 'Pavilion,' 'Crown,' and 'Table,' here's the reason...

When discussing faceted gems, the bottom is called the pavilion; the top section is called the crown; and the large facet on the top is called the table. We'll create each of these sections on a separate layer.

| pavilion | crown | table |

Now let's begin by creating the basic outline of the pavilion section.

To create the pavilion section

1 On the **Layers** tab, click on the **Pavilion** layer to make it the active layer. We'll construct the basic outline of the pavilion section of our gemstone.

2 On the left Drawing toolbar, on the QuickShapes flyout, click the ⬭ **Quick Ellipse**. Hold down the **Shift** key and draw a large circle, approximately 10 cm/4 inches in diameter, in the centre of your page.

If required, you can type exact dimensions on the **Transform** tab.

3 On the Quick Shapes flyout, click the ☆ **Quick Star**, then hold down the **Shift** key and draw a large star to fill the centre of your circle.

4 With the star selected, drag the node slider at the top of the shape to the right to create an eight-point star.

5 Press **Ctrl + A** to select both the circle and the star, and then click the **Align** tab.

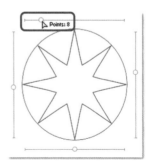

6 On the **Align** tab, select the **Include Page** check box and then click the **Horizontal Centre** and **Vertical Centre** buttons.

7 On the Drawing toolbar, click the **Straight Line** tool and draw a line from one side of the circle to the other, cutting through the star's points.

8 Repeat the previous step to draw three more lines and complete the shape as illustrated.

9 Press **Ctrl + A** to select all the objects, then to the right of the selection, click Group (or right-click and choose **Group**). We also rotated our grouped object by **22.5°** using the **Transform** tab.

We now need to create separate triangle and diamond shapes that we can fill. Click the **Zoom In** button on the HintLine toolbar to complete the following steps.

10 Click the **Straight Line** tool, then click a point where one of the line segments meets the outer edge of the circle (**Figure 1**, below).

11 Drag to trace the line down and click at the point where it meets the star shape (**Figure 2**). We've used a red line to illustrate the line tracing.

Drag back up to the circle's edge and click again. Close the shape by clicking again on the first node you created (**Figure 3**).

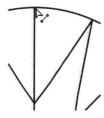

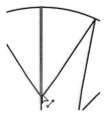

| **Figure 1** | **Figure 2** | **Figure 3** |

💡 Make sure that you have closed the shape by clicking back on the first node. If you have done so, you'll be able to apply a fill to the new shape created.

Figure 4

Finally, click the 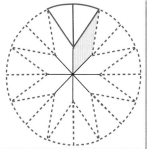 **Node** tool and then drag the top line so that it fits the curve of the circle's edge (Figure 4).

12 Select the triangle and press **Ctrl + C** to copy it to the Clipboard.

- Press **Ctrl + V** to paste a copy onto the page.

- On the **Arrange** tab, click ⚠ **Flip Horizontal** to create a mirror image of your original triangle.

- Rotate and move the copy into position next to the original, then select both shapes and click Group 📋 .

13 Copy the new group and paste it 7 times. Move the groups into position around the edge of the pavilion shape (illustrated in red).

14 Repeat steps 10 to 13 to create the diamond shapes (shaded in blue). When you have finished, you should have a total of 16 triangles and 8 diamonds.

Well done, you've completed the first section of your gemstone! (If you check on the Layers tab, you'll see all of your objects displayed in the tree hierarchy, under **Pavilion**.)

In the following section we'll create the gem's crown, and give you another chance to practise your skills with the **Line** and **Node** tools.

To create the Crown section

1   On the **Layers** tab, click on the **Crown** layer to make it the active layer.

2   On the Quick Shapes flyout, click the 🔘 **Quick Ellipse**, then hold down the **Shift** key and draw a circle exactly the same size as the one on your pavilion layer. You can check and alter the exact dimensions on the **Transform** tab. Position the circle directly on top of the pavilion shape.

3   With the circle selected, in the upper left corner of the **Colour** tab click the **Fill** button and then click the small grey and white swatch to the left of it. This removes the fill from the circle, allowing you to see the objects on the **Pavilion** layer beneath it.

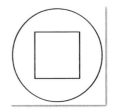

Now that we have the outline for our crown, let's hide the **Pavilion** layer so we're not distracted by it.

4   On the **Layers** tab, click the **Pavilion** layer's ◉ **Hide/Display Layer** button.

Your page now displays only the circle you just created on the **Crown** layer.

5   On the Quick Shapes flyout, click the ▭ **Quick Rectangle**, then hold down the **Shift** key and draw a square, approximately 5 cm/2 inches in size, in the centre of your circle.

6   Press **Ctrl + A** to select both objects, then on the **Align** tab, click 🖫 **Centre Horizontal** and 🔟 **Centre Vertically**.

🔖 When you first activate the **Crown** layer, you will still be able to see the shapes you created on the **Pavilion** layer. However, if you try clicking on them, you'll notice that you can't select these objects.

This is precisely why we're using separate layers in our document—the pavilion section we so carefully created is now safe on its own layer and we won't disturb it while we're working on the **other** layers.

7 Right-click the square and click **Copy**, then press **Ctrl + A** to select both items.

On the **Arrange** tab, select **45°** from the 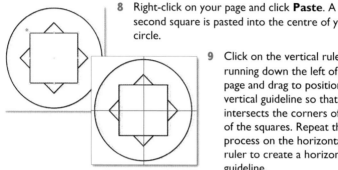 **Rotate**, drop-down menu.

8 Right-click on your page and click **Paste**. A second square is pasted into the centre of your circle.

9 Click on the vertical ruler running down the left of your page and drag to position a vertical guideline so that it intersects the corners of one of the squares. Repeat the process on the horizontal ruler to create a horizontal guideline.

10 Click the ⬛ **Straight Line** tool and use the ruler guides to help you draw lines from each corner of the square out to the circle's border.

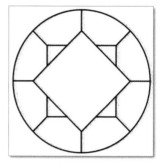

11 Select all the items on your page again (press **Ctrl + A**, or draw a rectangular selection box around all the items), then click 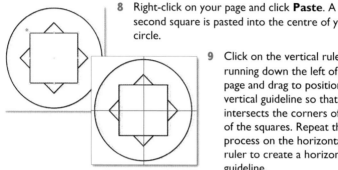 **Rotate (45°)**.

12 Repeat step 10 to connect the corners of the second square to the circle's edge.

You can remove the ruler guides now if you wish. To do this, just click on the guide and drag it back to the ruler.

13 On the QuickShapes flyout, click the **Quick Polygon** and draw a polygon on your page, outside of your circle (no need to hold the **Shift** key this time).

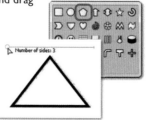

Drag the shape's upper node handle to the left to create a triangle.

14 Click the ◆ **Pointer** tool, then click on the triangle and drag it to a corner of one of your squares.

15 Resize and rotate the triangle so that its base sits between the corners of the two squares, and its apex extends towards the edge of the circle. (Using the **Pointer** tool, you can hover the pointer next to a node to temporarily switch to the Rotate cursor.)

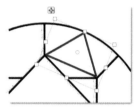

16 Resize and move the triangle so that it fits exactly between the corners of the squares and the border of the circle. You may need to zoom in to do this.

Now that our triangle is in place, let's use it as a guide to trace the outline of the facet.

17 Click the ◆ **Straight Line** tool and trace around the diamond shape that is formed by the top two sides of the triangle and the two edges of the squares.

Do not trace around the base of the triangle. (We've used a red line for illustration purposes.)

18 Copy and paste the new diamond shape, then use the method described in step 15 or the ◆ **Rotate** tool to move the shape into place in the next section of the circle, as illustrated. (At this point, you can also delete the "guide" triangle QuickShape created in step 14.)

19 Repeat the previous step to position six more diamond shapes.

20 Use the methods described in the previous section to create the remaining shapes—you should have 16 triangles around the outer edge of the circle; 8 small triangles at the points of the two squares; and an octagon shape in the centre.

21 Before moving on to the final layer, right-click the central octagon shape and click **Copy**.

To create the Table section

1 On the **Layers** tab, click on the **Table** layer to make it the active layer. Now hide the **Crown** layer by clicking the 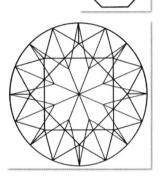 **Hide/Display Layer** button.

Your page should now appear blank.

2 On the **Edit** menu, click **Paste** to paste a copy of the octagon from your **Crown** layer on to your page.

3 On the **Layers** tab, display all the layers in your drawing by clicking the **Hide > Display Layer** button for the **Crown** and **Pavilion** layers. You should see something that resembles our illustration.

4 At this stage, you might want to save your drawing as a template—click **File > Save As** and save the file as **GemTemplate.dpp**. You can use this template later to create different coloured gems.

Next, we'll create a custom gradient fill to apply colour to our gemstone. We'll show you how to save your fill so that you can use it in future DrawPlus creations.

To apply and create a custom gradient fill

1 If you created a template file, close it now and reopen your original **Gem.dpp** file. We'll start by applying gradient fills to the pavilion of our gemstone, so make the **Pavilion** layer visible and the active layer, and hide the **Crown** and **Table** layers.

2 Select one of the shapes on the pavilion (you can use the ▚ **Pointer** tool or click a shape's thumbnail on the **Layers** tab).

3 On the **Swatch** tab, click the ▦ **Gradient** button, select the **Linear** category, and then click on any of the gradient fill swatches.

When you select a filled object, the 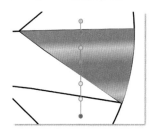 **Fill** tool becomes available (otherwise it's greyed out). If the object uses a gradient fill, you'll see the fill path displayed as one or more lines, with nodes marking where the spectrum between each key colour begins and ends.

Adjusting the node positions determines the actual spread of colours between nodes. You can also edit the fill by adding, deleting, or changing key colours. For more information, see online Help.

4   On the Drawing toolbar, click the ◈ **Fill** tool. You'll now be able to see the fill path and its nodes.

We want our gemstone to appear iridescent, so we'll edit the fill path and add colours that will create this effect.

5   On the **Swatch** tab, click on a colour swatch, and then drag over to a node on the fill path to replace the colour.

6   Repeat the previous step, dragging a selection of colours to the fill path until your fill looks something like ours.

⚠ Be sure the tip of the pointer is over the node or path (watch the cursor) when you release the mouse button. Otherwise the colour will be applied to the whole object as a solid fill.

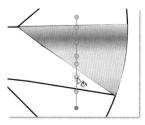

In addition to replacing colours on the fill path, you may also want to add some new colour nodes. To do this, simply drag from a colour swatch to a portion of the fill path where there is no node. A new node appears.

Let's now save this fill so we can apply it to other facets of the gemstone.

7   To save the fill, right-click, choose **Add to Studio**, then choose **Fill...** In the **Add Fill To Gallery** dialog, give your fill a name and click **OK**.

Add Fill To Gallery

Name Gem 01

OK

Cancel

On the **Swatch** tab, scroll down to see the swatch for your new custom gradient fill.

8   Click the 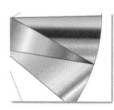 **Pointer** tool and select the shape you just filled. On the **Line** tab, click ⊞ **None** to remove the outline of the shape.

9   Select a different shape and fill it with any linear fill. Repeat steps 5 to 8 to create and apply another custom fill and remove the outline.

10 Repeat the previous steps to create a selection of custom fills for your gemstone's facets.

Make sure you vary the colours and the gradient of the fill path.

💡 If you don't want to create your own fills, you can copy ours from the **Gem.dpp** sample file. On the **stages of design layer**, right-click the fills we created and add them to your gallery.

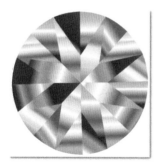

When you've applied your custom fills to all of the facets on the pavilion, it should resemble our illustration, left.

Let's now move on to the **Crown** layer...

To complete the gemstone crown

1   Hide the **Pavilion** layer and make the **Crown** layer visible and the active layer.

2   Apply your custom fills to the shapes on the crown and remove their outlines.

3   Draw a selection bounding box around the entire group of shapes (or press **Ctrl + A**), then on the **Colour** tab, change the **Opacity slider** to 50% opacity.

4   On the **Layers** tab, make the **Pavilion** layer visible.

You will now be able to see the pavilion through the semi-transparent crown.

Almost done! Let's move on and complete the table facet. Here, we'll simply be applying a gradient transparency to a white fill.

To complete the gemstone table and apply a gradient transparency

1   Make the **Table** layer visible and the active layer.

2   Apply a solid white fill to the shape and remove its outline.

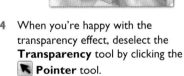

3   With the octagon selected, on the Drawing toolbar, click the  **Transparency** tool and draw a path from the edge of the octagon towards its centre.

You'll see that the shape becomes increasingly opaque as you move the node further towards the opposite side of the octagon.

4   When you're happy with the transparency effect, deselect the **Transparency** tool by clicking the **Pointer** tool.

You'll be glad to know that all the hard work is done and your gemstone is complete. Before we add the finishing touch, here's one last tip that you might find useful.

If your tracing skills are less than perfect, it's likely that some of your shapes and lines extend beyond the border of your circle. Don't worry, you can easily correct this by cropping your image.

To clip an object

1   On the **Layers** tab, make sure all your layers are visible and editable (click the 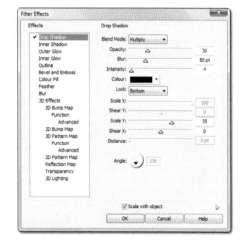 **Edit All Layers** button).

2   Select everything on the page (press **Ctrl + A**, or click **Edit/Select All**), right-click, and then click **Group**.

3   On the Drawing toolbar, click the **Crop** tool, and then on the context toolbar, select the **Circle** from the **Crop shape** flyout.

4   Drag the corner nodes inwards to resize your crop and remove any unwanted lines from your gemstone. (Pressing **Ctrl** while you drag will constrain the aspect ratio of the crop about the centre of the gemstone; **Shift** will allow you to change the shape of the ellipse.)

Your gemstone is now a perfect circle. You can make it look even more realistic by adding a drop shadow effect.

To create a drop shadow

1   Click to select your gemstone.

2   On the Drawing toolbar, click **Filter Effects**. In the **Filter Effects** dialog, select the **Drop Shadow** check box and set the following values:

- **Opacity:** 30
- **Blur:** 50
- **Intensity:** 4
- **Lock:** Bottom
- **Scale Y:** 35

(You can also use the **Shadow** tool to create and edit a drop-shadow 'on the page.')

Congratulations! You've created a gemstone from scratch. We've covered a lot of ground in this tutorial, and you should now be feeling more familiar with some of DrawPlus's powerful tools and features. We hope that you have enjoyed the exercise, and have learned a few things in the process.

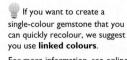 If you want to create a single-colour gemstone that you can quickly recolour, we suggest you use **linked colours**.

For more information, see online Help.

If you're feeling adventurous, open your **GemTemplate.dpp** file, save it with a different file name, and then try creating coloured gemstones by applying different linear fills. Or why not experiment with different shaped gemstones...

Creating a Wine Glass

Create a wine glass you can place on any background to show its transparency. We've created sample objects for you, but if you want to try this on your own you'll need to be (or become) familiar with the various line drawing tools.

You'll learn how to:

- Apply simple fills and transparencies using the **Swatch** and **Transparency** tabs.

- Use the **Transparency** tool to adjust the transparency of an object.

- Turn a basic line drawing into a realistic 3D image.

1 In the DrawPlus Startup Wizard, under **Open**, choose **Saved Work**, browse to the **...\Workspace** folder and open the **Wine Glass.dpp** file. In a standard installation, you'll find this folder in the following location:

C:\Program Files\Serif\DrawPlus\X3\Tutorials

The first page of the document shows a **keyline** (line drawing) of the wine glass, and the last page the finished article. In between pages are labelled in stages.

To navigate between pages, click the ◄ **Previous Page** and ► **Next Page** buttons on the HintLine toolbar.

2 Save the file under a new name, so you can work on it without altering the original.

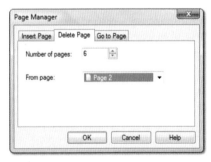

On the HintLine toolbar, click the 🗋 **Page Manager** and delete pages 2 to 7.

Reopen the original file and keep it available for reference while you're working on the other (use the **Window > Tile** command or adjust the windows for convenience).

For this tutorial we'll remove any elements that aren't required, and bring it all together at the end. We'll begin with the top of the glass and work our way down. Since the wine glass is in keyline form to start with, you will only be able to select an element by clicking on the line itself.

3 **(See Wine Glass.dpp, Stage *1*)** Click the keyline of the 'bowl' to select the shape that corresponds to *1* in **illustration A**. This shape has a light background colour.

  • On the **Colour** tab, apply a black fill and a set the **Opacity slider** to 10% opacity.

  • Remove the keyline (outline)—on the **Line** tab select ⊞ **None**.

4 Select the left 'strip glow' (labelled **2** in **illustration A**) and colour it solid white.

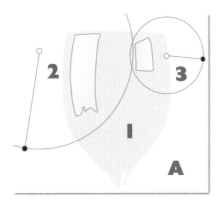

5 On the **Transparency** tab, in the ■ ▾ **Gradient** drop-down list, select **Radial** and apply a radial transparency (we used **Radial 21**). Use the 🔲 **Transparency** tool to adjust the transparency so its path looks like our illustration. Remove any keyline.

6 Repeat the previous step for the smaller strip glow (**A/3**).

7 **(See Stage 2)** Copy the strip glow 2 and paste it over itself—this trick gives a sharper transparency. Do the same with element 3, but after pasting it, nudge it slightly to the left. This will give the glass depth, as if light is reflecting from the inside as well.

8 Select the main bowl **(1)**, copy and paste it, then give it a white fill—it will be nearly invisible but that's the effect we want. Make it slightly smaller by pressing **Ctrl** while dragging inward on a corner handle.

🔖 We made the new 'clear' bowl slightly smaller than the original so that a bit of grey is revealed at the edges, lending a believable outline.

The bowl shape should now sit in front of the other bowl, hiding most of it. In **illustration B**, we've given the shape a false outline to illustrate its position.

In the next series of steps, we'll give this new bowl object some local transparency and then replicate it a number of times so it can contribute transparency in different places.

9   With the new bowl object selected, apply the **Ellipse 19** transparency.

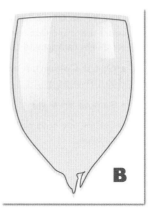

10 Click the ⬜ **Transparency** tool and using **illustration C/1** as a guide, position the transparency outside the object's right edge, slightly overlapping it to create a feathered soft edge. (In the illustration, the selection shows the overlap.)

In the overlap zone, you should see a blending into white where less transparency reveals the new bowl's white colour. We'll duplicate this object and adjust the transparency on each copy to extend the feathered edge.

11 Copy and paste the current bowl in place, then drag its transparency zone up so it affects the area labelled **C/2**.

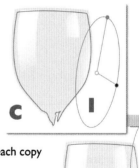

12 Repeat the paste operation and this time adjust transparency downwards to **C/3**.

Now you'll see a consistent white blend that follows the side of the glass. We'll use the same 'bowl' to add transparency in a couple of other areas.

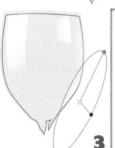

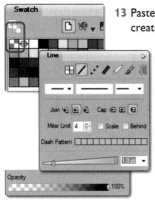

13 Paste the bowl again, but this time we will create a keyline as in **illustration D1**:

- remove the fill colour—on the **Swatch** tab, click to select the **Fill** swatch and then click the **None** swatch.

- apply a solid white line—on the **Line** tab, click the **Line** button and set the line thickness to 1pt. Then, on the **Swatch** tab, click to select the **Line** swatch and set the colour to white.

- set the opacity to 100%—on the **Colour** tab. drag the **Opacity slider** to the far right.

14 Drag the transparency (not the object!) up to the top left area, as shown in **D2**, and reshape it slightly to produce a light-reflective keyline that adds definition.

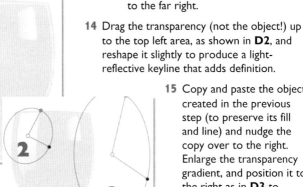

15 Copy and paste the object created in the previous step (to preserve its fill and line) and nudge the copy over to the right. Enlarge the transparency gradient, and position it to the right as in **D3** to create a stronger line down the side of the glass.

The next few operations are more of the same, in that we're adding a few more reflective transparencies—but these will be small 'flares' around the rim, front, side, and base of the glass. In **illustration E** we've coloured them black for emphasis, but yours will be white.

16 **(Stage 3)** For **E/1**, **E/2**, and **E/3**, create small white-filled circles with no line, flatten and stretch them as needed. Apply any elliptical transparency with resizing and adjustment to achieve the desired flare effects in very specific places.

17 For **E/4**, we used a simple radial transparency on a freehand shape.

18 At **E/5**, to finish off the top half, we added a small curved line that defines the base of the bowl. Applying transparencies to single lines is just the same as for shapes—in this case we used another elliptical transparency.

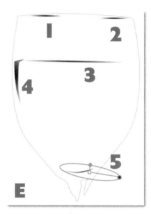

Against a coloured background, you should now have something closely resembling **illustration F**.

Now we'll follow similar procedures for the base and stem. The basic approach is to apply a light base colour and then side highlights, followed by the flares to add realism. We'll concentrate more on speed than detail, to avoid repetition. Don't forget to remove keylines unless otherwise stated. As in **illustration E**, we've illustrated the fills using black for emphasis, but yours will be white.

19 **(See Stage 4)** Select the keyline that defines the stem (**illustration G/1**), which will be using the original light background colour. Apply a black fill and solid 10% opacity. Copy and paste it in place, fill the copy with white, and add a 1pt white line.

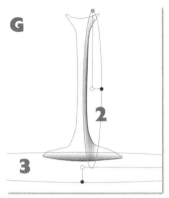

20 Using **G/2** as a guide, apply an elliptical transparency to the object and move the transparency (not the object) to the right of the stem, with a slight overlap. This effect will resemble what we achieved in **illustration C**.

21 Copy the object and paste it again, so it retains its white fill and line, then rotate the transparency and extend it to resemble **G/3**. This will give the base of the stem a reflective glow.

To finish off we'll apply the flares to the stem in the same manner we used in step 16 **(illustration E)**.

22 **(Stage 5)** You should still have a copy of the stem on the Clipboard, so paste it again and nudge it slightly to the right. Remove its fill colour but keep the white line. Apply a large radial transparency, similar in size to **G/2**, but circular, to get the effect as shown in **illustration H/1**. This should create a fine sliver down the left side of the stem, to give it more definition.

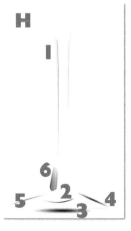

23 Copy and paste **E/5**, the line defining the base of the bowl, then drag the copy down to define the base of the stem where it starts to form the foot (**H/2**).

24 Repeat the copy/paste operation using the shape from **E/1**, moving this copy down to the very base and enlarging it to fill the full width as in **H/3**. Paste the same object again, and using **H/4** as reference place the copy to the right of the stem and rotate it to follow the contour. Repeat the paste-and-adjust step for **H/5**.

25 Finally, for **H/6** apply a radial transparency to the existing shape at that location, and move the transparency below and right so that the top of the shape is blended.

Congratulations! Now that you've mastered this technique, why not try applying the same methods to other objects like glass buttons for the Web; or use the skills you've learned to create shiny metallic objects and water effects.

The Gallery

This chapter showcases the content provided on the DrawPlus X3 **Gallery** tab. You'll find arts & crafts, cartoons, connecting symbols, layout symbols, shape art, and more.

Some of these elements are provided on the DrawPlus Program CD, others can be found on the Resource CD.

This chapter does not contain an exhaustive lost of all the categories and variations found in the DrawPlus gallery.

A

B

C

D

E

F

G

H

I

J

K

L

M

N

O

P

Q

R

S

T

U

V

W

X

Y

Z

Boy	Butterflies	Car	Dice	Fire
Flaming Bike	Flower	Girl	I Love You	Mod
Pop	Punk	Rainbow	Rock	Seal
Skull	Smile	Star		
Boggly Eyes	Buttons	Flower Beads	Furry Dogs	Furry Flowers
Furry Sun	Furry Teddies	Glass Beads	Jewels	Label

Note	Old Label	Page Corner	Page Curl	Paper

Paper	Paper Clip	Pin	Pin	Pin

Pink Note	Polaroid	Price	Price	Safety Pins

Sequins	Sticker	Tag	Tag	Tape Measure

Yellow Note	Yellow Note

Bird 1	Bird 2	Coffee 1	Coffee 2	Coffee 3

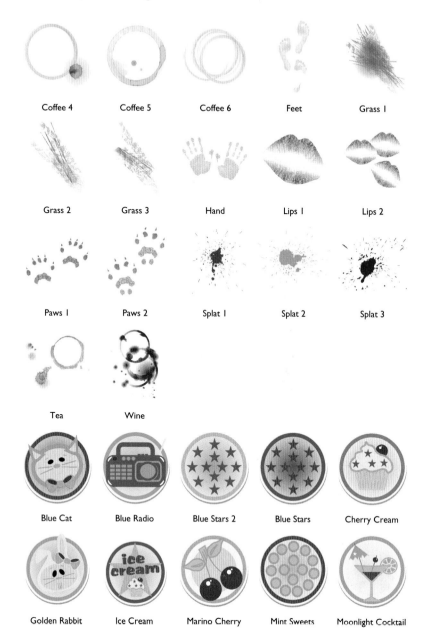

Coffee 4 · Coffee 5 · Coffee 6 · Feet · Grass 1

Grass 2 · Grass 3 · Hand · Lips 1 · Lips 2

Paws 1 · Paws 2 · Splat 1 · Splat 2 · Splat 3

Tea · Wine

Blue Cat · Blue Radio · Blue Stars 2 · Blue Stars · Cherry Cream

Golden Rabbit · Ice Cream · Marino Cherry · Mint Sweets · Moonlight Cocktail

Orange Cat

Orange Sweets

Party Cat

Party Rabbit

Raspberry Cat

Raspberry Radio

Red Rabbit

Star Cherry

Strawberry Cream

Sun Cocktail

Sunset Cocktail

Vanilla Cherry

Vanilla Cream

White Rabbit

Celtan

Crom

Gekkoz

Kung Fu

Mountain Goat

Pistolero

Smoking Gun

Spore

Squid

The Blade

Vision Quest

Warrior

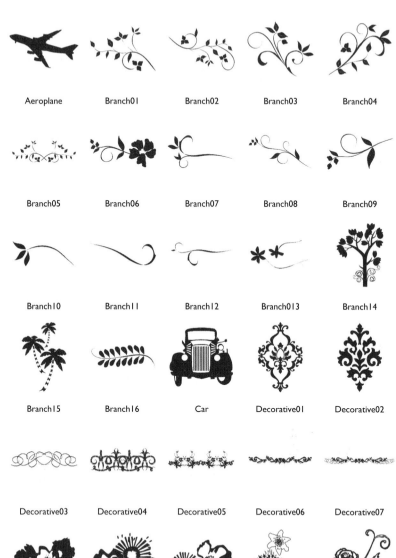

Aeroplane	Branch01	Branch02	Branch03	Branch04
Branch05	Branch06	Branch07	Branch08	Branch09
Branch10	Branch11	Branch12	Branch013	Branch14
Branch15	Branch16	Car	Decorative01	Decorative02
Decorative03	Decorative04	Decorative05	Decorative06	Decorative07
Floral01	Floral02	Floral03	Floral04	Floral05

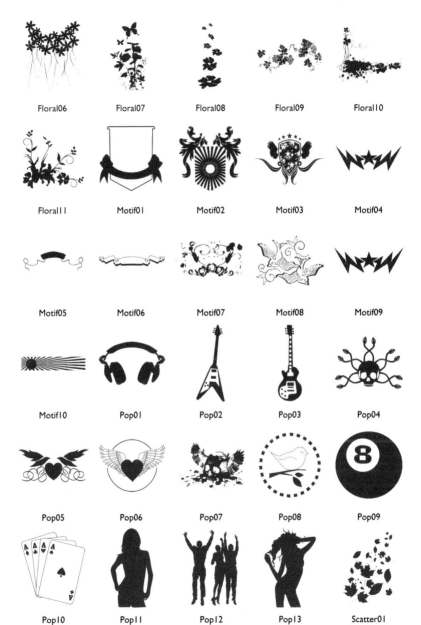

Floral06	Floral07	Floral08	Floral09	Floral10
Floral11	Motif01	Motif02	Motif03	Motif04
Motif05	Motif06	Motif07	Motif08	Motif09
Motif10	Pop01	Pop02	Pop03	Pop04
Pop05	Pop06	Pop07	Pop08	Pop09
Pop10	Pop11	Pop12	Pop13	Scatter01

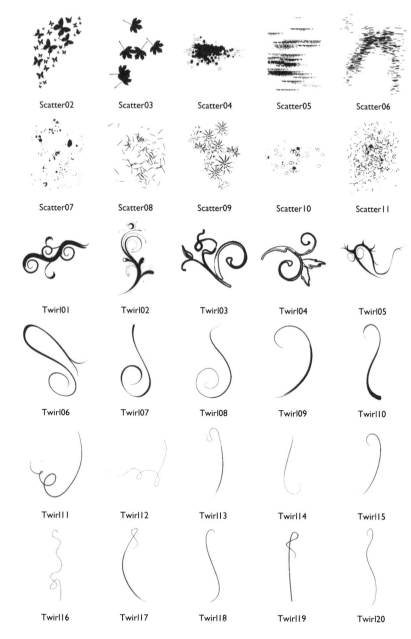

Scatter02   Scatter03   Scatter04   Scatter05   Scatter06

Scatter07   Scatter08   Scatter09   Scatter10   Scatter11

Twirl01   Twirl02   Twirl03   Twirl04   Twirl05

Twirl06   Twirl07   Twirl08   Twirl09   Twirl10

Twirl11   Twirl12   Twirl13   Twirl14   Twirl15

Twirl16   Twirl17   Twirl18   Twirl19   Twirl20

Bird	Bumblebee	Cow	Crab	Crocodile
Dinosaur	Dog	Donkey	Dove	Eagle
Elephant	Frog	Giraffe	Goldfish	Hamster
Hedgehog	Hippopotamus	Horse	Killer Whale	Ladybird
Lion	Lizard	Monkey	Mouse	Owl Baby
Owl	Penguin	Pig	Rabbit	Rat

Rhinoceros

Rooster

Shark

Sheep

Snake

Spider

Starfish

Tiger

Whale

Baby

Bib for Boy

Bib for Girl

Bootie

Bottle

Boy Girl Symbol

Pacifier

Rattle

Romper Suit

Teddy

Apartments

Apartments 2

Beach House

Church

Cottage

Factory

House

Mosque

Office

Power Station

Shack

Shop

The Clink

Tower Block

Tower Block 2

Ai - Love

Cai - Wealth

Fu - Good Luck

He - Harmonious

Lu - Prosperity

Shou - Longevity

Xi - Happiness

Angel 02

Angel

Baby Jesus

Bauble

Bell

Candle

Candy Cane

Christmas Tree

Christmas Trees

Cracker

Crown

Decorated
Christmas Tree

Elf

Fairy

Gift

Holly

Holly 02

Holly 03

Mistletoe 01

Mistletoe

More Christmas Trees

Orange Bauble 1

Orange Bauble 2

Penguin Fairy

Penguin on Tree

Penguin with Balloons

Penguin with Cake

Penguin Party Hat

Penguin and Tinsel

Polar Bear

Pudding

Purple Bauble 1

Purple Bauble 2

Purple Present

Red Present

Reindeer

Robin 02

Robin

Rudolph

Rudolph 2

Santa with Sack of Presents

Santa

Scroll Banner

Shepherd

Simple Tree

Snowman

Stocking 02

Stocking 03

Sugar Cane

Wise Man

Wreath 01

Wreath

Egg Basket

Flowers

Easter Bunny

Easter Duckling

Bathtime

Boots

Brush

Champagne Bottle

Champagne Glasses

Eyelash Brush

Flowers in Vase

Flowers

Gold Perfume Bottle

Green Perfume Bottle

Hair Brush

Hairdryer

Handbag

Hat

High Heels

Lipstick

Make-Up Brush

Mirror 1

Mirror 2

Perfume

Platform Shoes

Shoes

Shopping Girl

Slippers

Spray

01

02

03

04

05

06

07

08

09

10

11

12

13

14

15

16

17

18

19

20

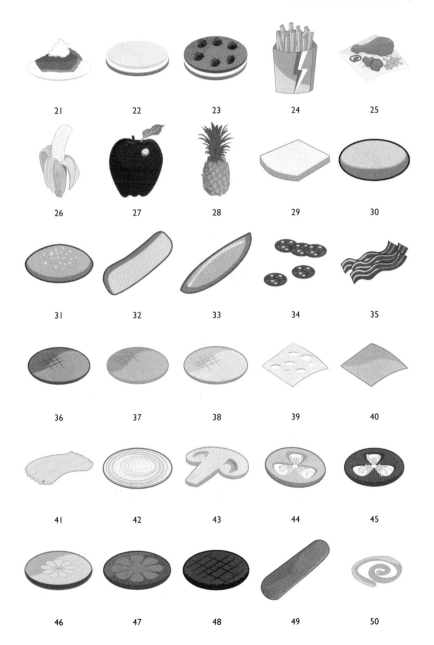

21   22   23   24   25

26   27   28   29   30

31   32   33   34   35

36   37   38   39   40

41   42   43   44   45

46   47   48   49   50

51

52

53

54

55

56

57

58

59

60

61

62

63

64

65

66

67

68

69

70

71

72

73

74

75

76

77

78

79

80

81

82

83

84

85

86

87

88

89

90

91

92

93

94

95

Angry Eyes

Army Helmet

Baby Bonnet

Blood-shot Eyes

Brown Beard

Cowboy Bandana

Cowboy Hat

Cute Eyes

Dracula

Ear Warmers

Ears

Elf Ears

Elf Hat

Frankenstein Bolts

Frankenstein

Hairdo I	Hairdo 2	Hairdo 3	Hairdo 4	Hypnotic Eyes
Lazy Eyes	Mexican Hat	Mexican Moustache	Native Indian Hairdo	Native Indian Headdress
Nose I	Nose 2	Nose 3	Pioneer	Pirate Hat and Eye Patch
Pirate's Parrot	Purple Beard	Sailors Hat	Scary Mouth I	Scary Mouth 2
Scary Mouth 3	Sheriff Badge	Silly Mouth I		
Fork	Hand Fork	Mower	Plant Pot	Pruner

Rake

Spade

Trowel

Archery

Artist Palette

Backpack

Ballerina

Boat

Boxing Gloves

Camera

Fishing Rod

Football

Footballer

Golf Bag

Horse Riding

Ice Skates

Karate

Skier

Snooker

Tennis

Balloons

Beachball

Bucket and Spade

Cake

Candle

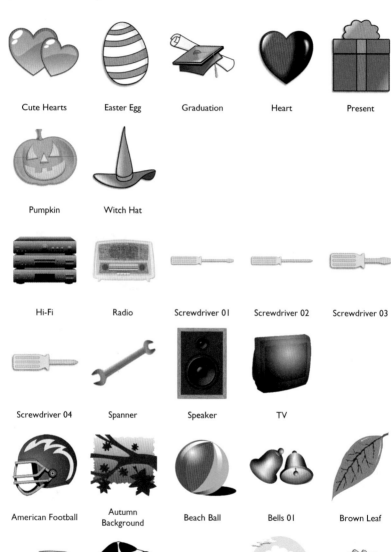

Cute Hearts

Easter Egg

Graduation

Heart

Present

Pumpkin

Witch Hat

Hi-Fi

Radio

Screwdriver 01

Screwdriver 02

Screwdriver 03

Screwdriver 04

Spanner

Speaker

TV

American Football

Autumn Background

Beach Ball

Bells 01

Brown Leaf

Car 02

Cat 02

Chopper

Clouds

Cogs

Easter Chick

Eggs

Fly

Flying Ant

Gear

Ghost

Graduation

Grass 01

Hammock

Hearts

Holly 01

Jet

Lizard

Melon

Motorcycle 02

Mountain Bike

Penguin

Pig

Pumpkin

Rabbit 02

Sandy Background

Shark

Snowball Skier

Snowman

Speedo

Strawberry

Steering

Straw Bale

Summer Background

Summer Daze

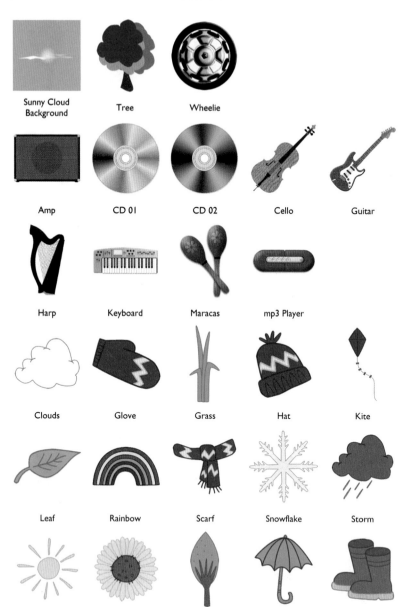

Sunny Cloud Background

Tree

Wheelie

Amp

CD 01

CD 02

Cello

Guitar

Harp

Keyboard

Maracas

mp3 Player

Clouds

Glove

Grass

Hat

Kite

Leaf

Rainbow

Scarf

Snowflake

Storm

Sun

Sunflower

Tree

Umbrella

Wellies

Balloon

Balloons

Bottle Cork

Champagne

Cupcake

Party Blower

Party Hat

Party Popper

Boy

Builder

Businessman 2

Businessman

Butler

Chef

Firefighter 2

Firefighter

Flower Girl

Girl

Golfer

Nurse

Police Officer

Policeman

Professor

School Boy

School Girl

Scientist

Secretary

Spaceman

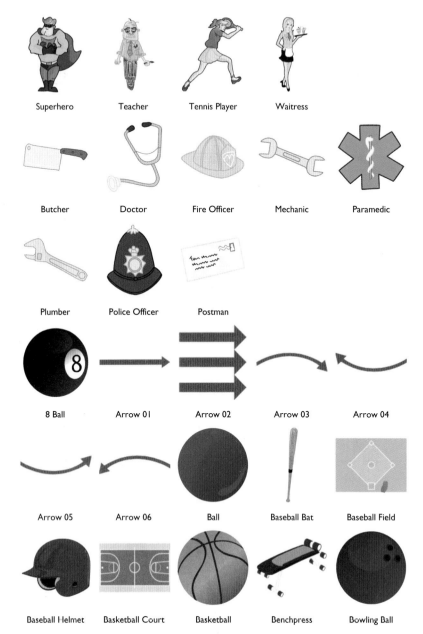

Superhero

Teacher

Tennis Player

Waitress

Butcher

Doctor

Fire Officer

Mechanic

Paramedic

Plumber

Police Officer

Postman

8 Ball

Arrow 01

Arrow 02

Arrow 03

Arrow 04

Arrow 05

Arrow 06

Ball

Baseball Bat

Baseball Field

Baseball Helmet

Basketball Court

Basketball

Benchpress

Bowling Ball

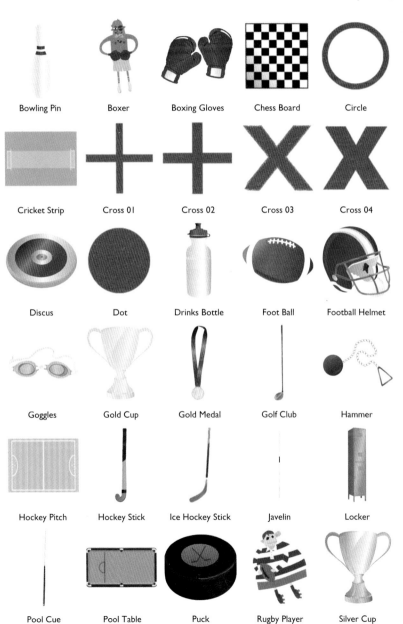

Bowling Pin	Boxer	Boxing Gloves	Chess Board	Circle
Cricket Strip	Cross 01	Cross 02	Cross 03	Cross 04
Discus	Dot	Drinks Bottle	Foot Ball	Football Helmet
Goggles	Gold Cup	Gold Medal	Golf Club	Hammer
Hockey Pitch	Hockey Stick	Ice Hockey Stick	Javelin	Locker
Pool Cue	Pool Table	Puck	Rugby Player	Silver Cup

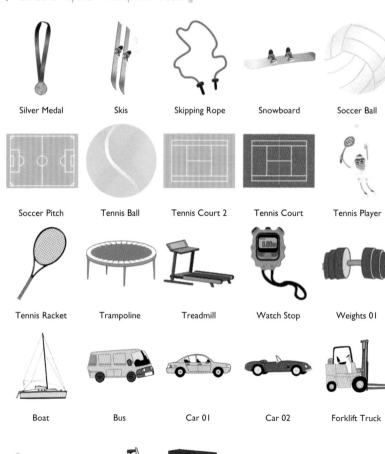

Silver Medal

Skis

Skipping Rope

Snowboard

Soccer Ball

Soccer Pitch

Tennis Ball

Tennis Court 2

Tennis Court

Tennis Player

Tennis Racket

Trampoline

Treadmill

Watch Stop

Weights 01

Boat

Bus

Car 01

Car 02

Forklift Truck

Jet

Scooter

Truck

Bells

Bouquet

Bride

Bridesmaid Dress

Cake

Church

Dress

Garter

Groom

Horseshoe

Just Married Sign.

Limousine

Top Hat

Bridge

Camera

Cell Phone

Comm-link

Comm-link_2

CRT

CRT_2

Ethernet

Fax

Firewall

Hub

Modem

PC Unit

Photocopier

Printer

Projector

Router

Scanner

Screen

Switch

Telephone

TFT

User

Video Camera

Wireless Router

Wireless

Antennas and Meters

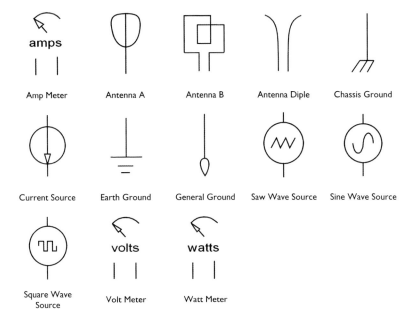

Amp Meter	Antenna A	Antenna B	Antenna Diple	Chassis Ground

Current Source	Earth Ground	General Ground	Saw Wave Source	Sine Wave Source

Square Wave Source	Volt Meter	Watt Meter

Cells and Connectors

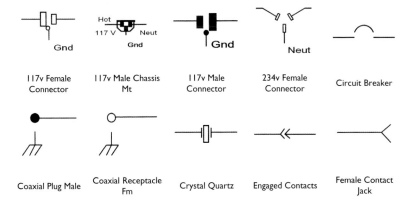

117v Female Connector	117v Male Chassis Mt	117v Male Connector	234v Female Connector	Circuit Breaker

Coaxial Plug Male	Coaxial Receptacle Fm	Crystal Quartz	Engaged Contacts	Female Contact Jack

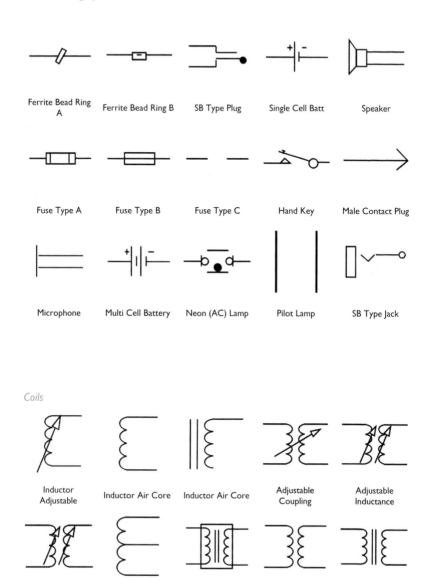

Ferrite Bead Ring A

Ferrite Bead Ring B

SB Type Plug

Single Cell Batt

Speaker

Fuse Type A

Fuse Type B

Fuse Type C

Hand Key

Male Contact Plug

Microphone

Multi Cell Battery

Neon (AC) Lamp

Pilot Lamp

SB Type Jack

Coils

Inductor Adjustable

Inductor Air Core

Inductor Air Core

Adjustable Coupling

Adjustable Inductance

Inductor Plug In

Inductor with Taps

Shielded w Iron Core

Transformer Air Core

Transformer Iron Core

Components and Logic Gates

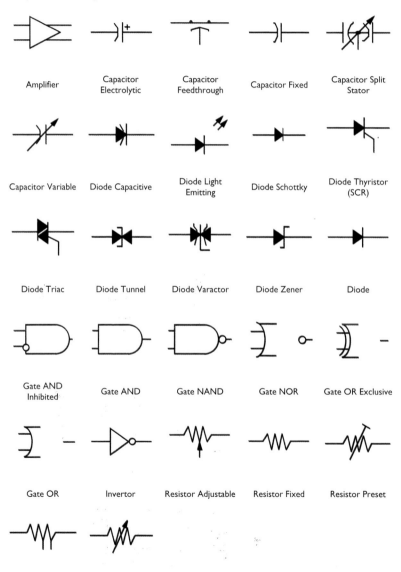

Amplifier	Capacitor Electrolytic	Capacitor Feedthrough	Capacitor Fixed	Capacitor Split Stator
Capacitor Variable	Diode Capacitive	Diode Light Emitting	Diode Schottky	Diode Thyristor (SCR)
Diode Triac	Diode Tunnel	Diode Varactor	Diode Zener	Diode
Gate AND Inhibited	Gate AND	Gate NAND	Gate NOR	Gate OR Exclusive
Gate OR	Invertor	Resistor Adjustable	Resistor Fixed	Resistor Preset
Resistor Tapped	Resistor Variable			

IC Chips and Crystals

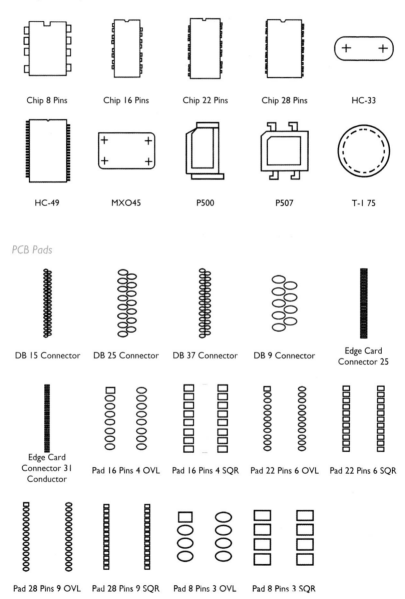

Chip 8 Pins   Chip 16 Pins   Chip 22 Pins   Chip 28 Pins   HC-33

HC-49   MXO45   P500   P507   T-1 75

PCB Pads

DB 15 Connector   DB 25 Connector   DB 37 Connector   DB 9 Connector   Edge Card Connector 25

Edge Card Connector 31 Conductor   Pad 16 Pins 4 OVL   Pad 16 Pins 4 SQR   Pad 22 Pins 6 OVL   Pad 22 Pins 6 SQR

Pad 28 Pins 9 OVL   Pad 28 Pins 9 SQR   Pad 8 Pins 3 OVL   Pad 8 Pins 3 SQR

Pin and Grid Array Sockets

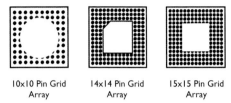

10x10 Pin Grid
Array

14x14 Pin Grid
Array

15x15 Pin Grid
Array

Sockets and Transistors

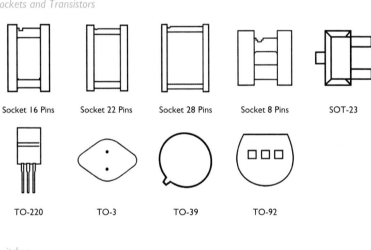

Socket 16 Pins   Socket 22 Pins   Socket 28 Pins   Socket 8 Pins   SOT-23

TO-220   TO-3   TO-39   TO-92

Switches

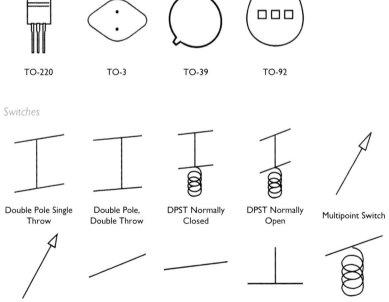

Double Pole Single
Throw

Double Pole,
Double Throw

DPST Normally
Closed

DPST Normally
Open

Multipoint Switch

Rotary Switch

Single Pole Single
Throw

Single Pole, Double
Throw

Slide Switch

SPDT Momentary

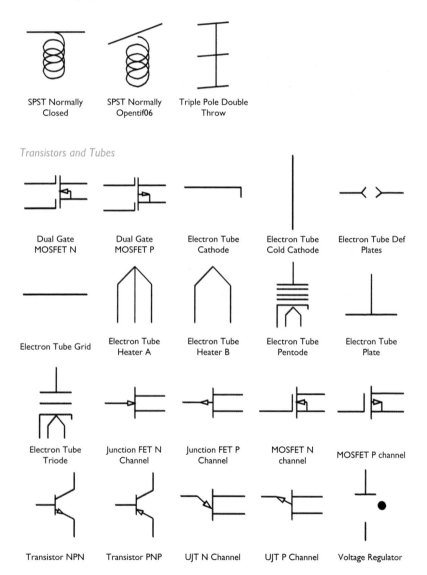

Transistors and Tubes

SPST Normally Closed	SPST Normally Opentif06	Triple Pole Double Throw		
Dual Gate MOSFET N	Dual Gate MOSFET P	Electron Tube Cathode	Electron Tube Cold Cathode	Electron Tube Def Plates
Electron Tube Grid	Electron Tube Heater A	Electron Tube Heater B	Electron Tube Pentode	Electron Tube Plate
Electron Tube Triode	Junction FET N Channel	Junction FET P Channel	MOSFET N channel	MOSFET P channel
Transistor NPN	Transistor PNP	UJT N Channel	UJT P Channel	Voltage Regulator

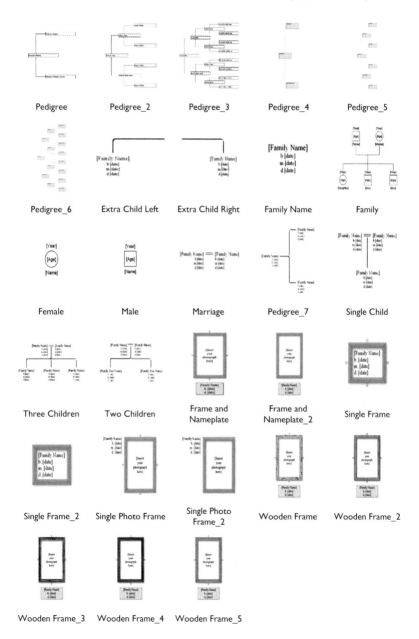

Pedigree   Pedigree_2   Pedigree_3   Pedigree_4   Pedigree_5

Pedigree_6   Extra Child Left   Extra Child Right   Family Name   Family

Female   Male   Marriage   Pedigree_7   Single Child

Three Children   Two Children   Frame and Nameplate   Frame and Nameplate_2   Single Frame

Single Frame_2   Single Photo Frame   Single Photo Frame_2   Wooden Frame   Wooden Frame_2

Wooden Frame_3   Wooden Frame_4   Wooden Frame_5

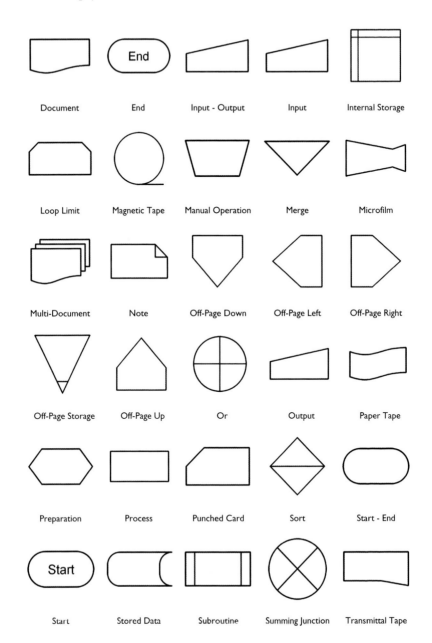

Document	End	Input - Output	Input	Internal Storage
Loop Limit	Magnetic Tape	Manual Operation	Merge	Microfilm
Multi-Document	Note	Off-Page Down	Off-Page Left	Off-Page Right
Off-Page Storage	Off-Page Up	Or	Output	Paper Tape
Preparation	Process	Punched Card	Sort	Start - End
Start	Stored Data	Subroutine	Summing Junction	Transmittal Tape

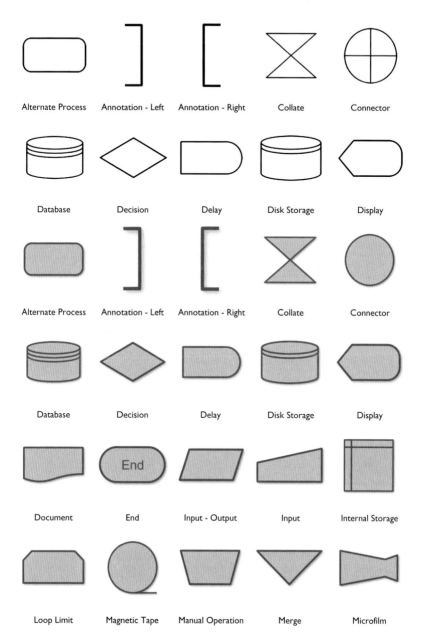

Alternate Process	Annotation - Left	Annotation - Right	Collate	Connector

Database	Decision	Delay	Disk Storage	Display

Alternate Process	Annotation - Left	Annotation - Right	Collate	Connector

Database	Decision	Delay	Disk Storage	Display

Document	End	Input - Output	Input	Internal Storage

Loop Limit	Magnetic Tape	Manual Operation	Merge	Microfilm

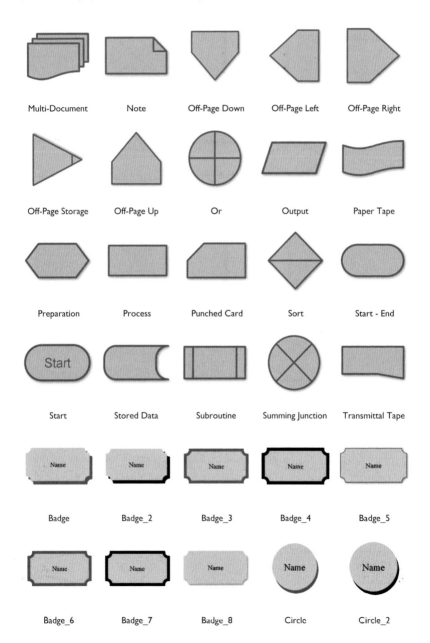

Multi-Document	Note	Off-Page Down	Off-Page Left	Off-Page Right
Off-Page Storage	Off-Page Up	Or	Output	Paper Tape
Preparation	Process	Punched Card	Sort	Start - End
Start	Stored Data	Subroutine	Summing Junction	Transmittal Tape
Badge	Badge_2	Badge_3	Badge_4	Badge_5
Badge_6	Badge_7	Badge_8	Circle	Circle_2

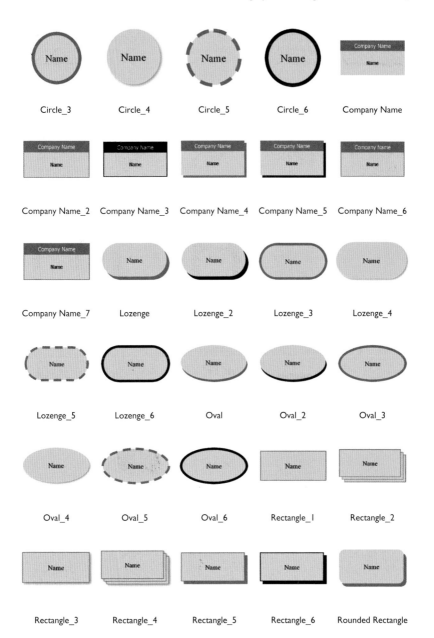

Circle_3	Circle_4	Circle_5	Circle_6	Company Name
Company Name_2	Company Name_3	Company Name_4	Company Name_5	Company Name_6
Company Name_7	Lozenge	Lozenge_2	Lozenge_3	Lozenge_4
Lozenge_5	Lozenge_6	Oval	Oval_2	Oval_3
Oval_4	Oval_5	Oval_6	Rectangle_1	Rectangle_2
Rectangle_3	Rectangle_4	Rectangle_5	Rectangle_6	Rounded Rectangle

Rounded Rectangle_2	Rounded Rectangle_3	Rounded Rectangle_4	Rounded Rectangle_5	Rounded Rectangle_6
Audio File	Audio	Blog	Blog_2	Client Side Script
Cloud	Database	Download	Download_2	Download_3
File	Form	FTP	Gopher	Hard Copy
Home Page	Home	HTML Page	Internet Terminal	Java Page
Jump Page	Mail To	Movie	News Group	News Group_2

News	News_2	Non-Secure Page	Non-Secure	Off Site Link
Page	Page_2	Page_3	Plug-in	R-Login
Search	Search_2	Secure Page	Secure	Server Side Script
Style Sheet	Telnet	Terminal	Web Page	Web Services
www	XML Page			

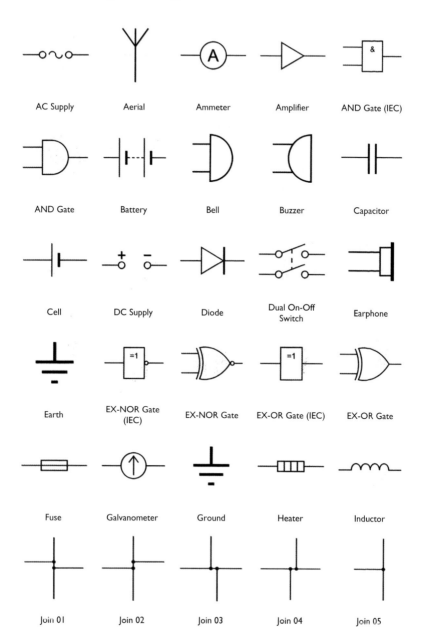

AC Supply

Aerial

Ammeter

Amplifier

AND Gate (IEC)

AND Gate

Battery

Bell

Buzzer

Capacitor

Cell

DC Supply

Diode

Dual On-Off Switch

Earphone

Earth

EX-NOR Gate (IEC)

EX-NOR Gate

EX-OR Gate (IEC)

EX-OR Gate

Fuse

Galvanometer

Ground

Heater

Inductor

Join 01

Join 02

Join 03

Join 04

Join 05

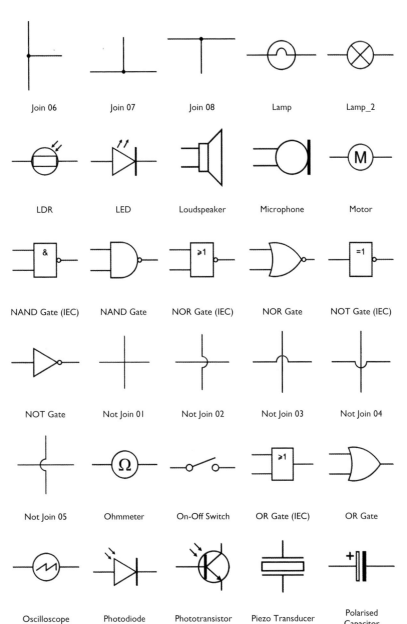

Join 06

Join 07

Join 08

Lamp

Lamp_2

LDR

LED

Loudspeaker

Microphone

Motor

NAND Gate (IEC)

NAND Gate

NOR Gate (IEC)

NOR Gate

NOT Gate (IEC)

NOT Gate

Not Join 01

Not Join 02

Not Join 03

Not Join 04

Not Join 05

Ohmmeter

On-Off Switch

OR Gate (IEC)

OR Gate

Oscilloscope

Photodiode

Phototransistor

Piezo Transducer

Polarised Capacitor

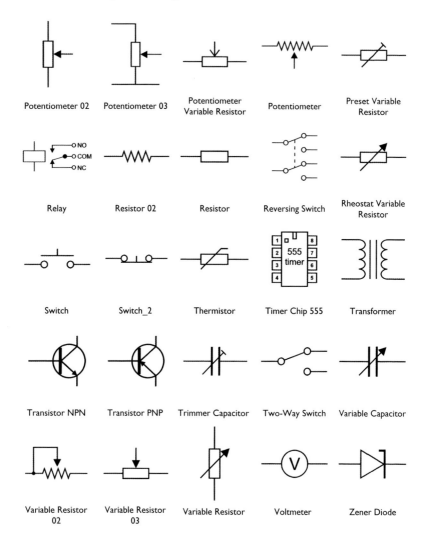

Potentiometer 02	Potentiometer 03	Potentiometer Variable Resistor	Potentiometer	Preset Variable Resistor
Relay	Resistor 02	Resistor	Reversing Switch	Rheostat Variable Resistor
Switch	Switch_2	Thermistor	Timer Chip 555	Transformer
Transistor NPN	Transistor PNP	Trimmer Capacitor	Two-Way Switch	Variable Capacitor
Variable Resistor 02	Variable Resistor 03	Variable Resistor	Voltmeter	Zener Diode

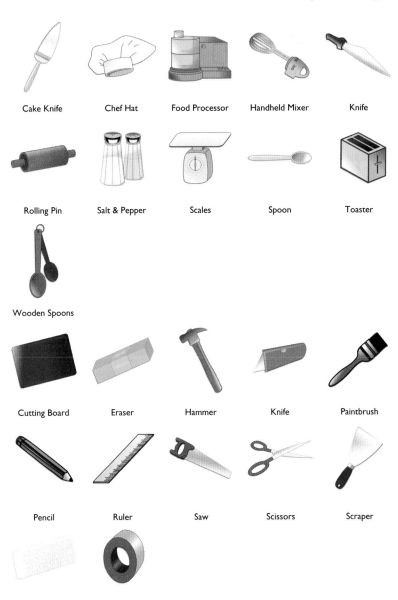

Cake Knife   Chef Hat   Food Processor   Handheld Mixer   Knife

Rolling Pin   Salt & Pepper   Scales   Spoon   Toaster

Wooden Spoons

Cutting Board   Eraser   Hammer   Knife   Paintbrush

Pencil   Ruler   Saw   Scissors   Scraper

Stationery Stencil   Tape

Austria

Belgium

Cyprus

Czech Republic

Denmark

England

Estonia

European Union

Finland

France

Germany

Great Britain

Greece

Hungary

Ireland

Italy

Latvia

Lithuania

Luxembourg

Malta

Netherlands

Poland

Portugal

Scotland

Slovakia

Slovenia

Spain

Sweden

United States of America

Wales

Bright Slight
Clouds

Clouds some
Sunshine

Cloudy - Night

Cloudy

Dark Clouds with
Rain - Night

Dark Clouds with
Rain

Dark Clouds

Fog - Night

Hazy

Heavy Rain

Icy Blizzard - Night

Icy Blizzard

Lightning Storm -
Night

Lightning Storm

Mild Sunshine

Showers - Night

Showers

Snow

Sunny Showers

Very Sunny

Snow - Night

Abacus 01

Abacus 02

pi

Protractor

Ruler

Set Square 01

Set Square 02

Abacus 01

Abacus 02

pi

Protractor

Ruler

Set Square 01

Set Square 02

Dna

Heart

Intestines

Lungs

Microscope

Retina

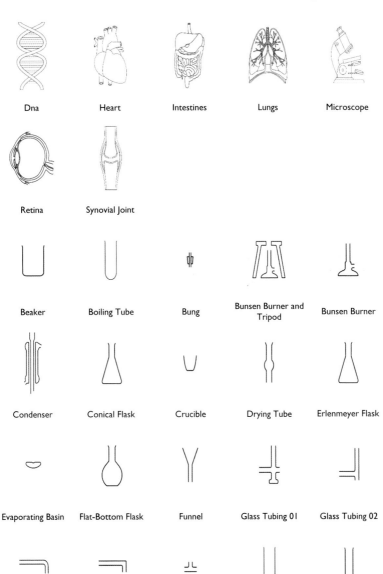

Dna

Heart

Intestines

Lungs

Microscope

Retina

Synovial Joint

Beaker

Boiling Tube

Bung

Bunsen Burner and Tripod

Bunsen Burner

Condenser

Conical Flask

Crucible

Drying Tube

Erlenmeyer Flask

Evaporating Basin

Flat-Bottom Flask

Funnel

Glass Tubing 01

Glass Tubing 02

Glass Tubing 03

Glass Tubing 04

Glass Tubing 05

Large Test Tube

Measuring Cylinder

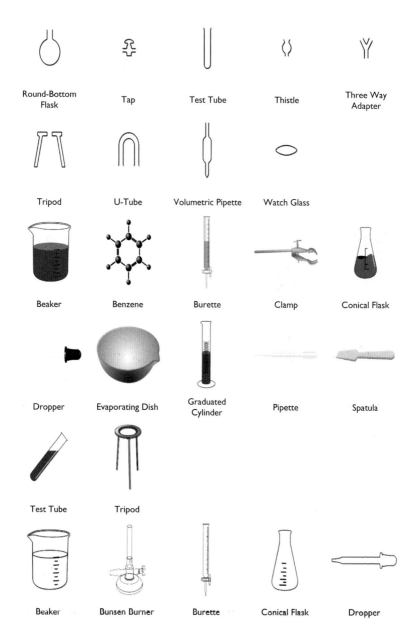

Round-Bottom Flask

Tap

Test Tube

Thistle

Three Way Adapter

Tripod

U-Tube

Volumetric Pipette

Watch Glass

Beaker

Benzene

Burette

Clamp

Conical Flask

Dropper

Evaporating Dish

Graduated Cylinder

Pipette

Spatula

Test Tube

Tripod

Beaker

Bunsen Burner

Burette

Conical Flask

Dropper

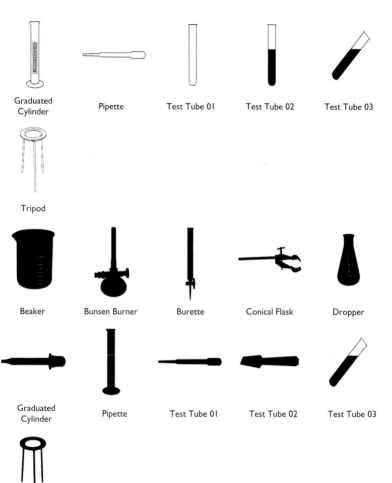

Graduated
Cylinder

Pipette

Test Tube 01

Test Tube 02

Test Tube 03

Tripod

Beaker

Bunsen Burner

Burette

Conical Flask

Dropper

Graduated
Cylinder

Pipette

Test Tube 01

Test Tube 02

Test Tube 03

Tripod

Atomic Structure

Blackboard
Formula

Magnet

Newton Cradle

Oscilloscope

Telescope

Atomic Structure

Blackboard Formula

Magnet

Oscilloscope

Baseball Pitch

Basketball Court

Chess Board

Cricket Pitch

Football Pitch

Hockey Pitch

Rugby Pitch

Snooker Table

Tennis Clay Court

Tennis Grass Court

Bench

Dumbbell

Skip Rope

Stop Watch

Trampoline

Treadmill

Weights

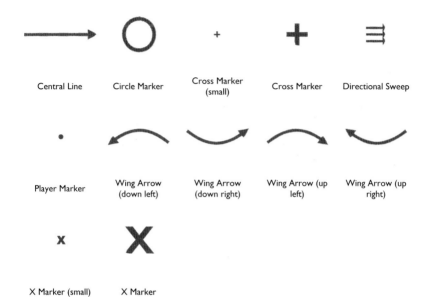

Central Line	Circle Marker	Cross Marker (small)	Cross Marker	Directional Sweep
Player Marker	Wing Arrow (down left)	Wing Arrow (down right)	Wing Arrow (up left)	Wing Arrow (up right)
X Marker (small)	X Marker			

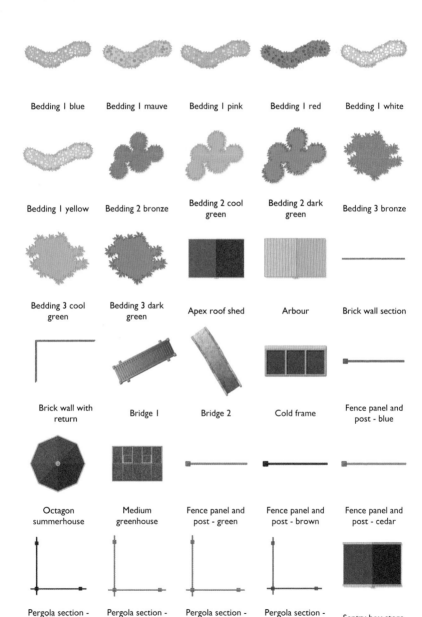

Bedding 1 blue

Bedding 1 mauve

Bedding 1 pink

Bedding 1 red

Bedding 1 white

Bedding 1 yellow

Bedding 2 bronze

Bedding 2 cool green

Bedding 2 dark green

Bedding 3 bronze

Bedding 3 cool green

Bedding 3 dark green

Apex roof shed

Arbour

Brick wall section

Brick wall with return

Bridge 1

Bridge 2

Cold frame

Fence panel and post - blue

Octagon summerhouse

Medium greenhouse

Fence panel and post - green

Fence panel and post - brown

Fence panel and post - cedar

Pergola section - brown

Pergola section - cedar

Pergola section - green

Pergola section - blue

Sentry box store

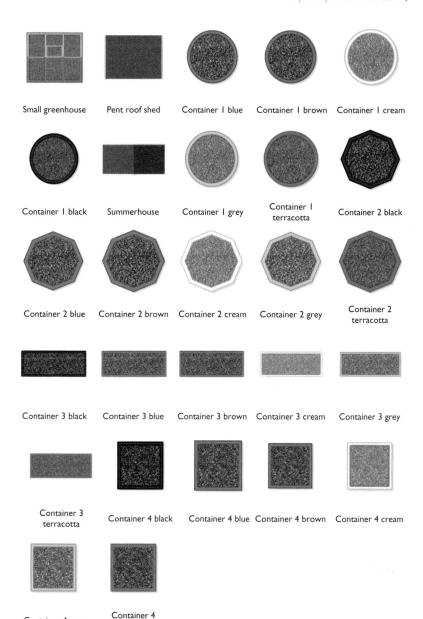

Small greenhouse

Pent roof shed

Container 1 blue

Container 1 brown

Container 1 cream

Container 1 black

Summerhouse

Container 1 grey

Container 1 terracotta

Container 2 black

Container 2 blue

Container 2 brown

Container 2 cream

Container 2 grey

Container 2 terracotta

Container 3 black

Container 3 blue

Container 3 brown

Container 3 cream

Container 3 grey

Container 3 terracotta

Container 4 black

Container 4 blue

Container 4 brown

Container 4 cream

Container 4 grey

Container 4 terracotta

Barbecue

Blue patio chair

Blue patio table 1

Blue patio table 2

Blue patio table 3

Blue patio table 4

Blue patio umbrella

Garden seat

Gnome

Green patio umbrella

Kid's slide

Natural patio chair

Natural patio table 1

Natural patio table 2

Natural patio table 3

Natural patio table 4

Sandpit

Teak patio chair

Teak patio table 1

Teak patio table 2

Teak patio table 3

Teak patio table 4

Terrace seating area - blue

Terrace seating area - natural

Terrace seating area - teak

Terrace seating area blue

Terrace seating area natural

Terrace seating area teak

Trampoline

Yellow patio umbrella

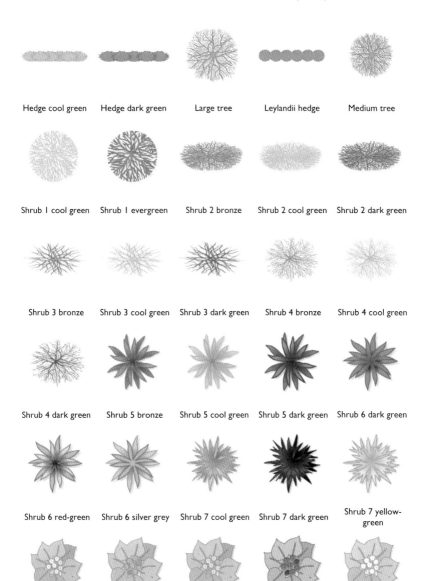

Hedge cool green	Hedge dark green	Large tree	Leylandii hedge	Medium tree
Shrub 1 cool green	Shrub 1 evergreen	Shrub 2 bronze	Shrub 2 cool green	Shrub 2 dark green
Shrub 3 bronze	Shrub 3 cool green	Shrub 3 dark green	Shrub 4 bronze	Shrub 4 cool green
Shrub 4 dark green	Shrub 5 bronze	Shrub 5 cool green	Shrub 5 dark green	Shrub 6 dark green
Shrub 6 red-green	Shrub 6 silver grey	Shrub 7 cool green	Shrub 7 dark green	Shrub 7 yellow-green
Shrub 8 blue	Shrub 8 mauve	Shrub 8 pink	Shrub 8 red	Shrub 8 white

Shrub 8 yellow

Shrub 9 bronze

Shrub 9 dark green

Shrub 9 pale green

Shrub 10 bronze

Shrub 10 cool green

Shrub 10 dark green

Small tree

Bark chip area

Bedding area 1

Bedding area 2

Bedding area 3

Bedding area 4

Bedding area 5

Bedding area 6

Bedding area 7

Border area 1

Border area 2

Border area 3

Border area 4

Coir matting section

Curved path section 1

Curved path section 2

Curved path section 3

Decking section blue

Decking section natural

Gravel area

Large pond 1

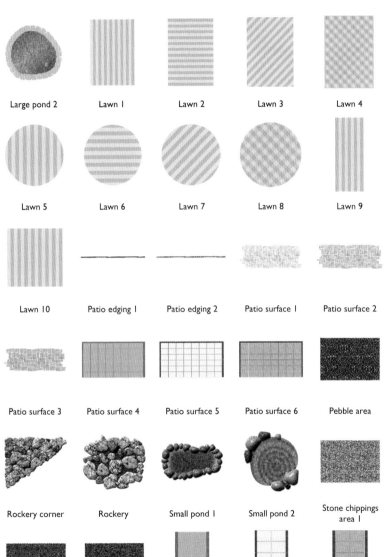

Large pond 2   Lawn 1   Lawn 2   Lawn 3   Lawn 4

Lawn 5   Lawn 6   Lawn 7   Lawn 8   Lawn 9

Lawn 10   Patio edging 1   Patio edging 2   Patio surface 1   Patio surface 2

Patio surface 3   Patio surface 4   Patio surface 5   Patio surface 6   Pebble area

Rockery corner   Rockery   Small pond 1   Small pond 2   Stone chippings area 1

Stone chippings area 2   Stone chippings area 3   Straight path section 1   Straight path section 2   Straight path section 3

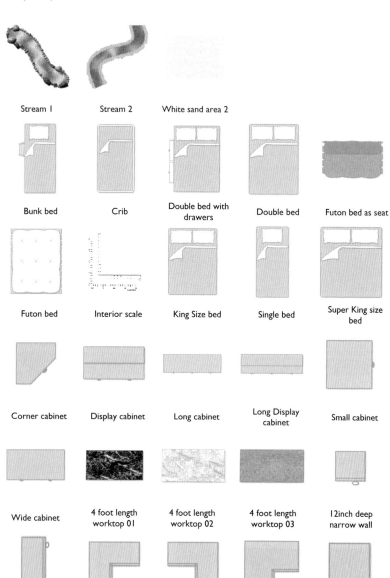

Stream 1

Stream 2

White sand area 2

Bunk bed

Crib

Double bed with drawers

Double bed

Futon bed as seat

Futon bed

Interior scale

King Size bed

Single bed

Super King size bed

Corner cabinet

Display cabinet

Long cabinet

Long Display cabinet

Small cabinet

Wide cabinet

4 foot length worktop 01

4 foot length worktop 02

4 foot length worktop 03

12inch deep narrow wall

12inch deep wall cabinet

12inch deep wall LHS corner cupboard

12inch deep wall RHS corner cupboard

20inch deep LHS wall corner cabinet

20inch deep narrow wall cabinet

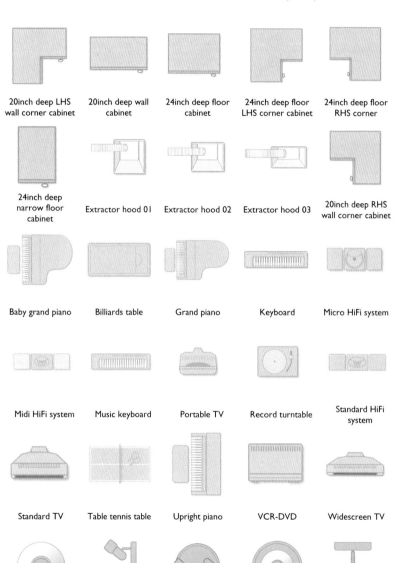

20inch deep LHS wall corner cabinet

20inch deep wall cabinet

24inch deep floor cabinet

24inch deep floor LHS corner cabinet

24inch deep floor RHS corner

24inch deep narrow floor cabinet

Extractor hood 01

Extractor hood 02

Extractor hood 03

20inch deep RHS wall corner cabinet

Baby grand piano

Billiards table

Grand piano

Keyboard

Micro HiFi system

Midi HiFi system

Music keyboard

Portable TV

Record turntable

Standard HiFi system

Standard TV

Table tennis table

Upright piano

VCR-DVD

Widescreen TV

Ceiling lamp

Double spotlight

Floor lamp with spots

Floor lamp

Low voltage spotlight

Low voltage track

Pendant light

Single spotlight

Uplighter

Wall lamp

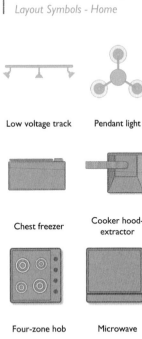

Chest freezer

Cooker hood-extractor

Cooker

Dishwasher

Five-zone hob

Four-zone hob

Microwave

Mini fridge

Range oven

Two-zone hob

Upright fridge-freezer

Washer or dryer

Belfast sink

Bidet

Corner bath

Corner bathtub

Corner shower 1

Corner shower 2

Corner sink

Double Belfast sink

Double drainer

Double sink with drainer

Double sink

Mixer taps

Oval bath

Oval bathtub

Round HotTub

Shower cubicle

Shower head unit front-on

Shower head unit

Sink mixer taps

Sink with left drainer

Sink with right drainer

Small bath

Small bathtub

Spacesaver sink

Square HotTub

Standard bath

Standard bathtub

Standard washbasin

Toilet with cistern

Toilet

Victorian bath

Victorian bathtub

Victorian washbasin

Walk-in shower

Armchair

Carver chair

Centre unit

DeLuxe recliner

Dining chair

Futon bed as seat

Left corner unit

Modular seating

Modular table

Recliner

Right corner unit

Settle

Three-seater settee

Three-seater sofa

Tub armchair

Two-seater settee

Two-seater sofa

4 place table

Oblong 6 place table

Oblong 8 place table

Oblong coffee table

Oval 4 place table

Oval 6 place table

Oval 8 place table

Oval coffee table

Round 4 place table

Round 6 place table

Round 8 place table

Round coffee table

12 foot wall

Bay window

Double doors

Double Floor Stairs

Double window

Single window

Spiral Staircase

Stairs

Standard door - left hand

Standard door - right hand

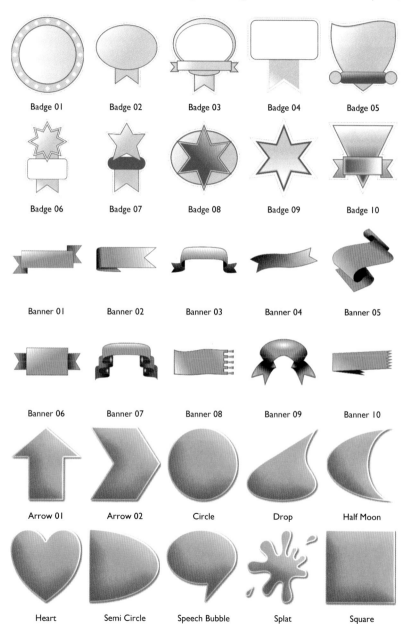

Badge 01   Badge 02   Badge 03   Badge 04   Badge 05

Badge 06   Badge 07   Badge 08   Badge 09   Badge 10

Banner 01   Banner 02   Banner 03   Banner 04   Banner 05

Banner 06   Banner 07   Banner 08   Banner 09   Banner 10

Arrow 01   Arrow 02   Circle   Drop   Half Moon

Heart   Semi Circle   Speech Bubble   Splat   Square

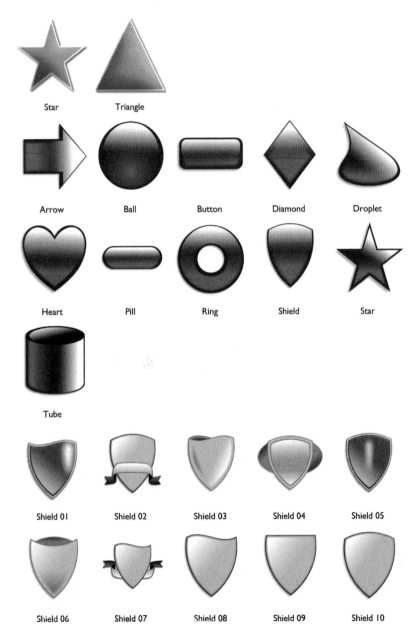

Star

Triangle

Arrow

Ball

Button

Diamond

Droplet

Heart

Pill

Ring

Shield

Star

Tube

Shield 01

Shield 02

Shield 03

Shield 04

Shield 05

Shield 06

Shield 07

Shield 08

Shield 09

Shield 10

Angry

Cheeky

Cool

Crying

Duh

Gormless

Grin

Rich

Romantic

Sleepy

Surprise

Scribble 01

Scribble 02

Scribble 03

Scribble 04

Scribble 05

Splat 01

Splat 02

Splat 03

Splat 04

Splat 05

Splat 06

Splat 07

Splodge 01

Splodge 02

Splodge 03

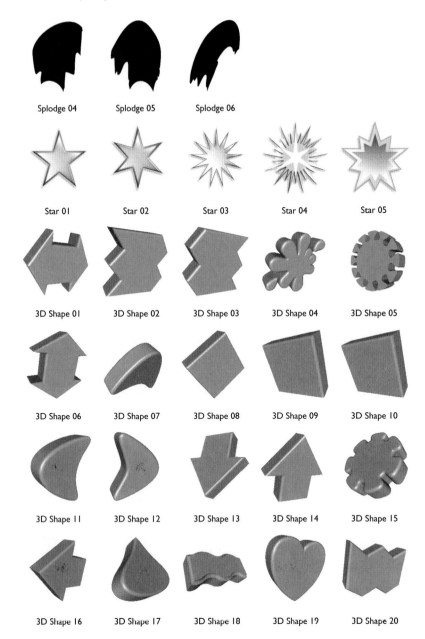

Splodge 04   Splodge 05   Splodge 06

Star 01   Star 02   Star 03   Star 04   Star 05

3D Shape 01   3D Shape 02   3D Shape 03   3D Shape 04   3D Shape 05

3D Shape 06   3D Shape 07   3D Shape 08   3D Shape 09   3D Shape 10

3D Shape 11   3D Shape 12   3D Shape 13   3D Shape 14   3D Shape 15

3D Shape 16   3D Shape 17   3D Shape 18   3D Shape 19   3D Shape 20

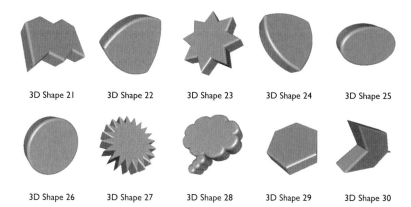

| 3D Shape 21 | 3D Shape 22 | 3D Shape 23 | 3D Shape 24 | 3D Shape 25 |
| 3D Shape 26 | 3D Shape 27 | 3D Shape 28 | 3D Shape 29 | 3D Shape 30 |

Design Templates

This chapter provides a reference gallery of the design templates included on the DrawPlus Resource CD.

The design templates can be accessed from the Startup Wizard and include **Arts & Crafts**, **Education**, **Logos**, **Posters**, **Web Banners**, and **Greeting Cards** categories. Be sure to check out the keyframe animation design templates in the **Animated Web Banners** category!

The **Arts & Crafts** category includes Pop-up Cards, Colouring In, Cootie Catchers, Paper Crafts, Scrapbooking, and Wrapping Paper. All of these templates are interactive and ready for you to print out and use.

Where necessary, we have provided illustrations of how the templates will look when printed out, cut out, and folded.

Champagne

Flowers

Halloween

Headphones

True Love

Space Aliens

Farmer

Ice Cream

Pirates

Cootie Catchers

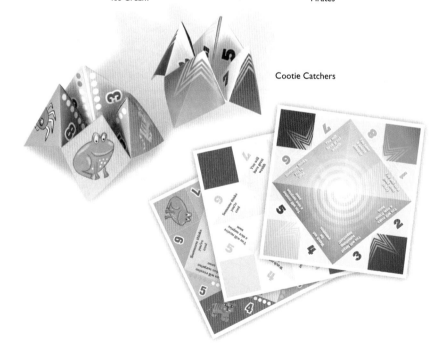

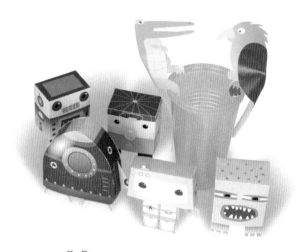

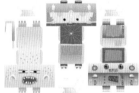

Box Toys

Cocktail Characters

Space Toy

Nursery Mobiles

Shuttle

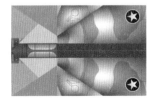

Jet Plane

Camping

Messy Desk

Blue Stripes

Flowers

Hearts

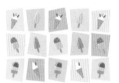

Ice Cream

Kids

Modern

Petals

Pink Crackle

Space

Periodic Table

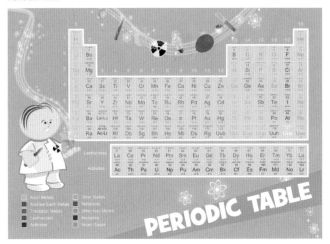

Alphabet Chart

Balanced Diet

School Play.

Secondary School Class Timetable

African Art Show

Book Store

Classic Car Show

Coffee Morning

Country Folk

Dance Event

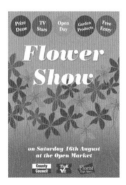

Flowers Show

Folk Festival

Garden Festival

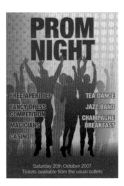

Prom Night

Record Fair

Record Sale

Village Fair

Butterfly Menu

Cafe Now Open

Dancing Club

Drinks Offers

Italian Restaurant

Lounge Club

Party Club

Restaurant Open Soon

Action Movie

Car Sales

City At Night Movie

Education Crafts

Environment Notice

Looking For Love Movie

Performance Management
Training

Sci-Fi Movie

Closing Down

Cruise Offer

Discount Swirly

Dressmakers

Everything Dropped

Fine Wines

Flower Bouquet

Fresh Skin Care

Music Shop

New Year Sale

Open Day

Organic Cosmetics

Shirts Spring Deals

Splash Out

Spring Sale Motif

Store Banner

Summer Collection

Sunglasses Offer

The Fruit Tree

Tropical Holidays

Urban Alternative Retail

Web Banners

The **DrawPlus X3 Design Templates** include **Animated Web Banners and Static Web Banners** sections.

Both animated and static web banners are easy to insert into and modify on your own Web pages!

Web Banners - Animated

Animated Web Banners are **keyframe animation** documents—our example below illustrates various stages of the animation—why not open one and preview it for yourself?

Digital Media

Chocoholics

College

Green Solutions

Holiday Adventures

Outdoors

Red City

Regina

Restaurant

Tricore

College

Chocoholics

Epoc Solutions

Outdoors

Restaurant

Web Hosting

Animals

Casino

Digital Camera

Digital Media

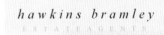

Estate Agents

Green Solutions

Health & Beauty

Lunar Eclipse

Martial Arts

Music

Orange Orb

Tricore

Web Hosting

Wine

xytron

Animals

Casino

Digital Camera

Digital Media

Estate Agents

Green Solutions

Health & Beauty

Lunar Eclipse

Luxury Hotel

Martial Arts

Music

Orange Orb

Tricore

Web Hosting

Wine

xytron

Animals	Bees	Dinosaur	Elephants	Footballer
Frog	Gardener	Guitar	Motorbike	Party
Rugby	Sunflower	Tennis	Trees	Bauble
Christmas Cheer	Christmas Pud	Christmas Puddings	Mistletoe	Nativity
Robin	Santa	Snowflakes	Snowman	Abstract Canvas

Baby Boy

Baby Girl

Ballerina Thanks

Be My Valentine

Champagne

Circles

Congratulations Wedding Cake

Cute Hearts

Easter Egg

First Day at School

Get Well Soon Teddy

Graduation

Halloween

I Love You

I'm Sorry

Just Married

Leaving Rooster

Mothers Day

New Arrival Bunnies

Passed Driving Test

Relax

Retirement

Sorry

Thank You

Brushes

DrawPlus provides an exciting range of possibilities for creating artistic effects using natural media effect brushstrokes, spray brushes, coordinated themed palettes, and instant effects.

Brushes tab: Provides new and improved pressure-sensitive brush strokes for creating natural media effects. You'll also find a selection of new spray brushes, including airbrushes, smoke, and clouds, which you can use to create impressive effects (see *Chapter 5, Samples* for examples).

Get to grips with these design elements and you'll dramatically expand your potential for creativity!

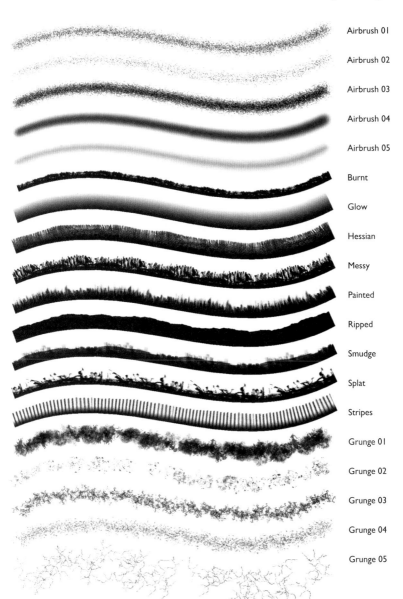

Airbrush 01

Airbrush 02

Airbrush 03

Airbrush 04

Airbrush 05

Burnt

Glow

Hessian

Messy

Painted

Ripped

Smudge

Splat

Stripes

Grunge 01

Grunge 02

Grunge 03

Grunge 04

Grunge 05

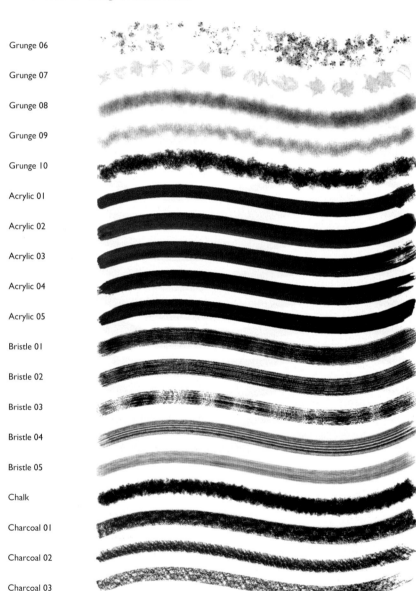

Grunge 06

Grunge 07

Grunge 08

Grunge 09

Grunge 10

Acrylic 01

Acrylic 02

Acrylic 03

Acrylic 04

Acrylic 05

Bristle 01

Bristle 02

Bristle 03

Bristle 04

Bristle 05

Chalk

Charcoal 01

Charcoal 02

Charcoal 03

'Chalk Tree' sample made using the Natural Media Chalk brush.

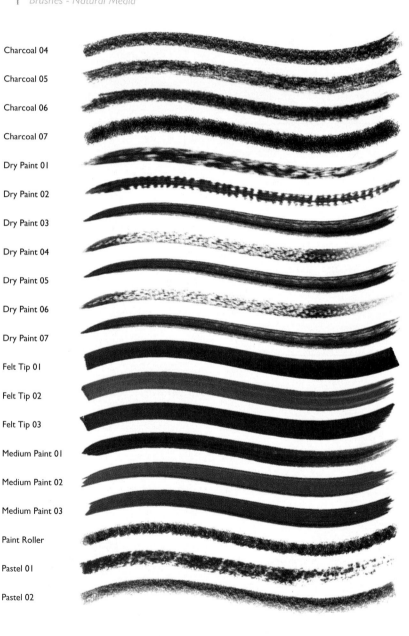

Charcoal 04

Charcoal 05

Charcoal 06

Charcoal 07

Dry Paint 01

Dry Paint 02

Dry Paint 03

Dry Paint 04

Dry Paint 05

Dry Paint 06

Dry Paint 07

Felt Tip 01

Felt Tip 02

Felt Tip 03

Medium Paint 01

Medium Paint 02

Medium Paint 03

Paint Roller

Pastel 01

Pastel 02

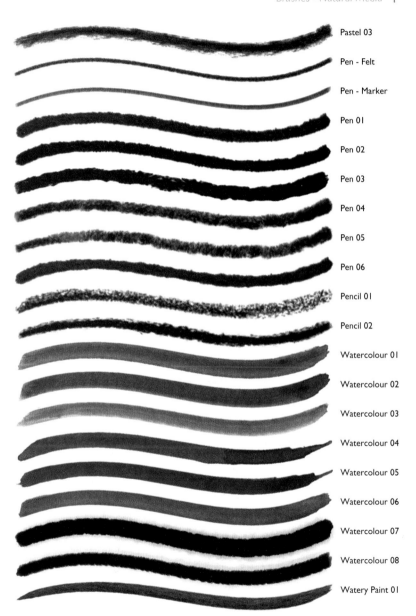

Pastel 03

Pen - Felt

Pen - Marker

Pen 01

Pen 02

Pen 03

Pen 04

Pen 05

Pen 06

Pencil 01

Pencil 02

Watercolour 01

Watercolour 02

Watercolour 03

Watercolour 04

Watercolour 05

Watercolour 06

Watercolour 07

Watercolour 08

Watery Paint 01

This sample was made using the Candy brush.

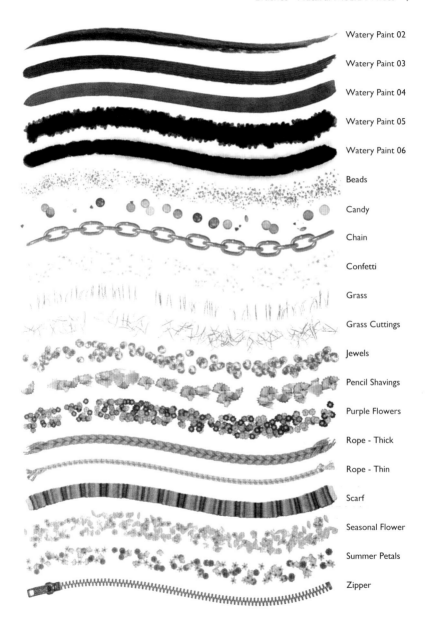

Watery Paint 02

Watery Paint 03

Watery Paint 04

Watery Paint 05

Watery Paint 06

Beads

Candy

Chain

Confetti

Grass

Grass Cuttings

Jewels

Pencil Shavings

Purple Flowers

Rope - Thick

Rope - Thin

Scarf

Seasonal Flower

Summer Petals

Zipper

'Teddy' sample made using the Special Effects Teddy Bear brushes.

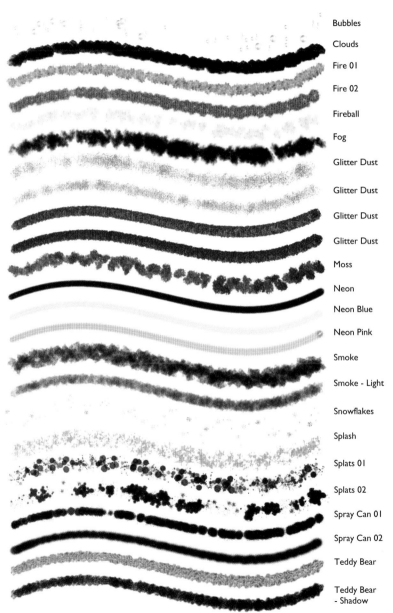

Bubbles

Clouds

Fire 01

Fire 02

Fireball

Fog

Glitter Dust

Glitter Dust

Glitter Dust

Glitter Dust

Moss

Neon

Neon Blue

Neon Pink

Smoke

Smoke - Light

Snowflakes

Splash

Splats 01

Splats 02

Spray Can 01

Spray Can 02

Teddy Bear

Teddy Bear
- Shadow

Default 01

Default 02

Default 03

Default 04

Default 05

Default 06

Default 07

Default 08

Default 09

Default 10

Default 11

Default 12

Default 13

Threadless 01

Threadless 02

Threadless 03

Threadless 04

Various Colours -01

Various Colours -02

Various

Various

White 01

White 02

White 03

White 04

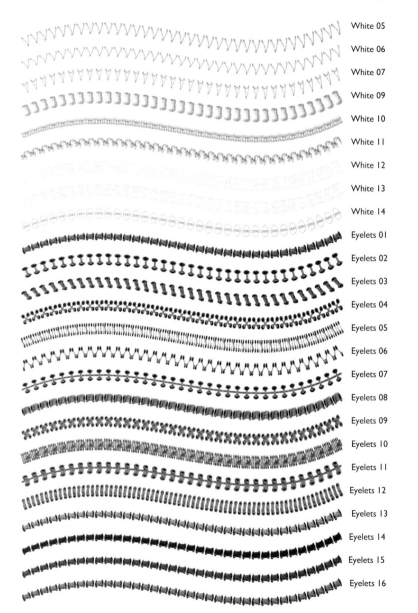

White 05
White 06
White 07
White 09
White 10
White 11
White 12
White 13
White 14
Eyelets 01
Eyelets 02
Eyelets 03
Eyelets 04
Eyelets 05
Eyelets 06
Eyelets 07
Eyelets 08
Eyelets 09
Eyelets 10
Eyelets 11
Eyelets 12
Eyelets 13
Eyelets 14
Eyelets 15
Eyelets 16

Samples

To demonstrate the incredible flexibility of DrawPlus, we've provided you with a varied collection of sample documents.

The samples include realistic media effects created with the natural media brushes, impressive cloud and smoke effects created with the new spray brushes, and a varied selection of posters and animations.

We hope they'll inspire you to create your own works of art!

Chalk Tree

Charcoal Elephant

Cloudy Night

Fireball

Grunge Brushes

Pastel Still Life

Pears

Teddy Bear

Watercolour
Flowers

Watercolour
Sunrise

Watercolour Tree

Dancing Club

Dressmakers

Ice Cream

Party Club

Pirates

Village Fair

Alien Alone

Bruiser George

Come Back Soon

Concert Poster

Floral Escape

Go Ski

Little Devil Bill

Mum Son and Dog

Sports Car

Office DayDream

Portrait

Robot Convention
2020

Space Boys

Space Child

The Tree of Forgotten Guilt

Watercolour

Pastel City

Bird on a Rock

Bridge

Dog

Electricity

Fishing

Still Life

Toucan

World Window

Bass Synth

Bike

Drinks On Us

Electric Fan

Golf

Radio Days

Shark

Technical

Watch2

Scooter

Jigsaw

Boxes

Cat Running

Lamp

Watch

'Fireball' sample made using the Special Effects brushes.

'Watercolour Sunrise' sample made using the Natural Media brushes.

'Charcoal Elephant' sample made using the Natural Media brushes.